Tryst with Divinity

Dr. Preeti Batra

Invincible Publishers

First published in India in 2018

ISBN: 978-93-88333-00-9

Invincible Publishers

G-120, Sushant Lok III, Sector 57, Gurgaon-122002

Registered Address: Opposite Kasturba Ashram, Radaur, Haryana - 135133

Printed at Thomson Press (India) LTD

Dedicated to

"DIVINE LOVE"

Acknowledgement

The book "Tryst with Divinity" is the proof of unconditional love. A love that has not been experienced to date. It's a privilege to acknowledge my gratitude to God's blessings. All experiences and sequences narrated in this book happened to be instructions from his unseen hands. Whenever there was even an inkling of a doubt, it got cleared within a few moments. Tryst with Divinity has freely flown in its present form. Thank you, Dear Lord, for your love, support, and for choosing me to make "Tryst with Divinity".

Contents

Chapter 1

Aristocratic life

The scorching sun was turning orange and cool in the twilight. Birds were retiring to their feathery nests and so were the wanderers trudging back home. Life is merry for many; and murky for more. It is difficult to describe life in a few words. Mother Nature, as we witness, can be munificent and devastating.

This generous flow of life is evident at "Pratibha Niwas", a palatial bungalow with spacious lawns. The razzmatazz inside the house flaunted the festivities that were going on. People on the street were openly talking about the pompous lifestyle of the aristocratic family living in the mansion. How can someone be so energetic and flamboyant after crossing the age of sixty! Unbelievable! With the businessman of the year award and many more achievements to his credit, he was a maverick since the beginning and was gifted with a charismatic personality. Nature bestowed him name, fame, and money which he accepted gracefully. He could turn his depressed mood to a sprightly one almost instantly. He was powerful enough to influence anyone. The mere appearance of this legend would humble the public and yield submission. He loved to be cajoled by the fulsome men around him. It is all about Mr. Rajit Lal, the business tycoon with a magnetic personality, anything said is less about him.

He had a compact and combined family of three children-Karan, Varun, and Avantika. All married and living with him with their individual families in the same spacious bungalow. The untimely demise of his beloved wife a few years ago was the most unfortunate event in his life. After his wife left for eternal abode leaving him terribly distressed, he started shifting his focus towards creating wealth and earn fame and respect.

Gossip and rumours were the appetizing contents of any party and Pratibha Niwas, where all Page 3 celebrities had congregated, was no exception. It is needless to blame people for being envious of Mr. Lal's achievements. The empowerment and the success of the suave personality of Mr. Lal were truly commendable. There was much talk about the press conference too which was to be held inside the hall. The party was going on in the open lawns. The media people were busy finishing their snacks before they went to attend the scheduled press conference. All the news channels were ready for the live coverage of the extravaganza.

"I think I should go and call Papa," Karan muttered near Latika's ears. A highly sceptical Karan Lal was the eldest son of Mr Lal. His wife Latika owned a boutique that exclusively catered to the high society wardrobe. That day, she had worn a slinky outfit. She turned back and nodded her head in consent.

"Wait for a while, bhaiya", Pallavi, Varun's wife who was an interior designer by profession, interrupted Karan, "Varun has already gone to Papa's room to call him."

"Oh! Pallavi, you better be with Latika. I'll join you in a few minutes", saying so Karan rushed hurriedly to Mr Lal's room.

The two co-sisters gazed and smiled at each other casually and exchanged pleasantries. "Nice saree, Pallavi! You must have gone to one of those middle-class shops you love so much to buy it. But for such grand parties, you should have dorned some designer outfit." The casual remark passed by Latika disturbed Pallavi, but, as usual, she took the things light-heartedly and walked off to Avantika who had just entered the party with her husband, Saurabh.

***

"Hello, Avantika, you're looking beautiful and elegant in this Indo-Western dress! Your pendant too is so attractive and how perfectly it is complementing your outfit!"

"Thank You Pallavi," Saurabh responded before Avantika could respond, "Avantika, I am going to Dad's room," saying so, he rushed to Mr Lal's room.

"Your saree is very pretty, Bhabhi. I must say you have a very nice taste. That is why Varun Bhaiya was caught at first sight."

Pallavi couldn't understand and wondered how to respond to the coarse comment and the compliment as well. She just smiled at and got off on the pretext of associating with other guests. Her's was a love marriage and, unlike Latika, she belonged to a middle-class family. She resented the 'high-cultured' society and hence was hardly be amiable with anyone. She always felt a bit confused with the relations where,' who was who and to whom' was hardly known. Everything was a show-biz and everyone wore a façade in that so-called elite society where relationships were viewed as though they were corporate balance sheets. Finance and social status were the criteria for building relations. It is no exaggeration that money played the primary role in everyone's lives. Pallavi, for sure, could not have taken differently even the views of her family too. She was not unaware of why Mr. Lal was always surrounded by a large group of people. The party continued in the open lawns even after it got dark. People were eagerly awaiting Mr. Lal in the hall along with the media personnel who were already seated inside. After a little while, Mr. Lal entered the hall with his large entourage. The gathering in the hall obsequiously greeted them with a loud applause. Even at that mature age, the vibrant persona appeared as a prodigy. A quietude prevailed in the hall for a short while and everyone was inquisitive and were waiting to listen to his message.

"Good Evening, Ladies and Gentlemen," Mr. Lal began. There was a huge round of applause. This echo of the welcoming accolades penetrated his heart. He had always received grand welcomes where ever he visited. Ecstatically, he continued, "I am endorsing a new range of bio-organic foods, cosmetics, and textiles. We are planning to expand and penetrate both into the domestic and international markets as well as introduce a new range of products which are scarce in the market. As we have established a brand image of our own for all our goods, I believe this new range too would stand up to the image in the respective sectors of the industry. We look forward to your support as ever, in our…………………………end………..eavour .

On……….behalf………………o…..f…….wa…ter………wa…te …r …"

"Papa, Papa!" Karan called out in panic, rushed to him, and tried to offer him water.

Mr. Lal sounded words as scattered letters and struggled to speak. The swirling tempest of words inside his mouth gushed out with a whizzing sound as his face squeezed awry. Soon the doyen of the corporate world collapsed, having suffered a cataleptic stroke. His brain was benumbed and his senses ceased functioning momentarily. It looked as if the period was highly hostile to him, upsetting his fortunes at the moment.

Live coverage of the entire sequence of the legend getting paralytic was covered by the media as "breaking news". The entire world watched the news, some in pain, some in vain, some in wonder, and some for fun.

Mr. Lal soon became unconscious and the shocked family took him to a hospital. Everyone, including the media, was anxious about his health and prospects of recovery. He was kept in I.C.U. The doctors advised the family to stay calm, assuring no threat to life, and that they could take him home after he regains consciousness. They also mentioned with regret and hesitation that the right part of his body **was paralyzed and would need special care till he recuperated fully.**

Such is the course of life, unpredictable, uncertain, and full of surprises. At times it is adorable and at times it is abhorrent. Life, that had been so generous to Mr. Lal up until now, had given him a bash. It looked that people had got a new topic for discussion. No one in this world can relish happiness all through life, that's an axiomatic truth. When news spread all over, many were reminded of the proverb 'Man proposes and God disposes'. The unfortunate paralytic stroke suffered by Mr. Lal became the talk of the town for quite some time.

Chapter -2
The Agony

Mr. Lal was brought home after a few days. The last couple of days had been no less than a nightmare for him. It was hard for him to accept the harsh realities of life as he had lived a hectic and lively life. Though proper arrangements were made to look after him, accepting life in this pathetic condition was not that easy for such a man. He felt invidious of his dependence on others to go through his routine and natural chores of life. A nurse and an attendant had been arranged to serve him round the clock. A doctor would visit daily for a health check-up and observed the progress made. All modes of treatment like physiotherapy, home spa, acupressure etc. were being tried for a rapid progress.

"My riches can buy me anything but not sleep and peace of mind," he lamented. His swollen sleepless eyes kept looking towards the roof most of the time. Thoughts flew aimlessly in Mr. Lal's mind, he felt depressed and moody. He was deeply disheartened for living in a humiliating cage wherein his mind, body, and soul were suffering from excruciating pain. The people who surrounded him once all the time had deserted him and now he was left all alone.

"It's time for your medicine, Sir," the nurse's voice reached his ears. He opened his mouth with immense difficulty and the nurse administered his medicine and left while he anxiously moved his eyes around to locate if anyone were there. Alas! There was no one. They would visit only once in a day as a formality. What a paradox life is! Things we think our own are not truly ours, even our body and our children. In his contemplative mood, he ruminated the past. "Do we own anyone?" he thought.

Interrupting his flow of thoughts, the attendant came with a bedpan and asked him to relieve himself and he helplessly obeyed and soon went into deep sleep under the sedative effect of the administered medicines.

"Today is my birthday, Karan," Latika whispered. They were in their bedroom.

"How can you be so insensitive, it has not even been two weeks to the tragic incident and you are planning for a grand party?" Karan replied, annoyed at her.

"Don't repeat it, Karan," Latika retorted. "We are page-3 people and no tragedy can stop us to go ahead in life. Be practical and regain confidence as we have to resume our routine sooner or later. Let us not refrain from celebrating functions and arranging get-togethers. Let us go ahead with celebrating my birthday. We can invite the chosen people and the media. The publicity and the acclaim you receive would be all yours, according to the 'Power of Attorney' given to you by your father."

"I think you are right." Karan was convinced with his wife's deciding tone.

In the other bedroom, things were another way around.

"Pallavi, "Varun said," I think we should go and ask my father our share in business and property. Things are turning for the worse at the office and I am unable to tolerate Karan's bossy attitude. He pokes his nose in my decisions. I have noticed Latika's domineering talk too with you. Why don't you retaliate?"

"No, Varun, relationships can't be measured, they are to be valued. We should respect the value of a relationship."

"It is basically the different CRPs that make us think differently," Pallavi thought.

"What happened? Where are you lost?" Varun asked.

"Leave it," Pallavi muttered and said, "Why do you want to ask papa about your share when he is going through such a bad phase of life?"

"Dear, if we don't talk on this issue then the other two will make the best deal of it. In this world, money is power and I want to be powerful," Varun replied.

"God knows what are you up to!" Pallavi succumbed to her husband's demands.

Avantika and Saurabh too talked on the same lines.

Love was transforming itself into its most deleterious form - jealousy. It started polluting the atmosphere of the house and generating negative energy. Selfish and confrontational feelings were surfacing. Negative energy had seized everyone leading to hostilities and incoherent thoughts. The enervated Mr. Lal failed to understand the apathetic attitude of his children towards him. His endurance and forbearance levels were at their peak but were getting weakened by the influence of the disturbed vibrations. These vibrations work mystically and a single thought would suffice to create energy, whether positive or negative. Pratibha Niwas was stuck by this lethal ghost.

"Is papa awake?" Avantika's voice cut through the silence. After getting consent from the nurse, she entered his room. Mr. Lal opened his eyes. Avantika was shocked to see the hollowness that was prominent in his eyes.

"Papa, you've been such an inspirational source for all of us. I can't see you like this. You just take care of your health. Don't think too much about business. I think Saurabh can very well take care of your new project and carry it on further," saying so, she looked at him for his consent.

Mr. Lal slowly closed his eyes and his thoughts entered the negative territory. Everyone wanted him to abdicate, while he was still alive!

"Papa, Papa," Avantika tried to talk but he didn't respond. She understood his silent response and had left silently with a heavy heart.

It was not his fault. When a person faces a prolonged physical illness, he becomes very sensitive towards himself. Mr. Lal saw himself as a victim and people around as culprits. Even if someone tried to sympathize with him, they seemed wily. His execrable imaginations would leave him more depressed and sleepless. His unbridled thoughts would devour his peace and deteriorated his health even further. He became much more sensitive than ever before. Avoidance and escapism became his tools. He was not willing to confront his children. He was scared of the questions he expected from his children that would torment him further, like say, "Who will be the next successor?" He had started resenting the presence of his children.

He was awakened from his slumber due to loud guffaws and merry chatter coming from outside. He opened his eyes and wondered what was happening. The nurse understood his inquisitiveness and told him about the party that was going on in the hall. It was Latika's birthday party. This was another jolt to his thoughts and he began to feel further dejected. He suffered physical pain and mental agony beyond the tolerable limits.

"What a humiliating life I'm living! No one in the house bothered to even tell me about the party." His heart was filled with hurt, it was broken and shattered. He wanted to retaliate but was emaciated. The physical weakness and the mental trauma he was suffering forced him to search for the flaws in relationships. "Is it that the relationships are meant for good times only? Everyone was so attached to me when I was fine, but no one gave me company during the saddest phase of my life," he muttered. He felt dejected and deserted even by his own beloved children whom he had nurtured and reared with utmost care and love as his dearest and invaluable assets.

His dinner plate remained unattended on the side table. Truly, there was no feeling of hunger in him and was in deep torment.

Chapter-3

A strange dream

Five months passed like this. There was some improvement in Mr. Lal's condition. By now he had probably accepted his fate and his family accepted him to be captious. However, he was happy that he could at least sit on a wheelchair and breathe fresh air in his huge lawn. One day, after his meal he expressed his wish to the attendant to take him out. While passing through the corridor, a chortle hit his ears. He stopped to eavesdrop. Latika's voice was very clear, "Hey stop your jokes, Varun. It's high time to ask about Dad's strange attitude. He can't ignore us like this."

"You're right, Bhabhi," said Varun, "I think we should go and ask for partition."

"What! Partition!?" Karan said, "Are you out of your mind, Varun? I think we should talk to him about his successor in the business."

Mr. Lal told his attendant to take him back. "Oh! These people are conspiring against me. I will not condone this. My children are not worried about me. They just want my power. Why don't they understand that they are inept to take care of such a huge empire? I don't see even a single person who is capable so I can hand over my business. It took me ages to build all this. I cannot see its ruins in front of my eyes. This is all mine. I will not give it to anyone. And to my children, never!" While lying on the bed, his eyes got stuck on the roof and his thoughts fluttered. He closed his eyes & slipped into the arms of subconsciousness.

He was standing in a dark room. As he opened the windows, he saw the mesmerizing beauty of nature. The Rising Sun, the morning dew, the chirping birds, the sturdy mountains and a sparkling waterfall in the middle of a vast green land. A pious light originated from the sky, which entered his room but was a few steps away from him. Calm, soothing breeze touched him and he saw his arms willing to embrace the pious light. As he tried to move, he realized that his feet were tied in a rusty, jumbled iron chain. To his surprise, he did not try to free his feet with his hands which were free. He saw he was helpless but calm. He was bogged down due to the sense of bondage.

With a sudden shock, he opened his eyes. What was that? A dream! Why were my feet tied but the arms free? I could have easily freed my feet but why couldn't I? What a beautiful scene it was! As if a parasol of peace had come to soothe me. Mr. Lal felt thirsty and wanted something to slake his thirst. After drinking water, he snuggled on his bed and enjoyed his snooze after a long time.

Avantika entered the house. "Here, madam comes again," Latika couldn't stop thinking.

Vibrations move faster than anything. Avantika responded in her thoughts, "Don't get disturbed by my coming here. After all, I am the daughter of the house."

Both exchanged warm gestures, keeping the heat inside. "How is Papa now? Is he still behaving the same, Latika?"

As if Avantika had touched the Pandora box, Latika lamented, "Oh Dad! We're scared of going to his room these days. As if we' visit, he'll again be unconscious. I believe it is best to avoid him by pretending to be unwell."

Avantika felt irritated by Latika's remark. "Anybody at his place would behave the same, Latika. I think we should give him that space."

Oh! You mean to say we don't understand his problems? At this age, he wants to work as if he was in his forties. His body is posing constraints before him. We just want to share his responsibilities. But he is hell-bent to not trust us. Do you think we're wrong?"

"Don't put words in my mouth. Everybody knows what exactly you want." The argument was becoming heated.

Karan & Varun entered the house. That put doused the heat for the time being.

Both brothers looked tensed and tired. "Latika, can you arrange for the drinks? We'll dine later on," Karan requested.

"O.K. Radheyshyam, open the bar for Sahib," Latika ordered.

"Is everything fine, bhaiya?" Avantika enquired.

Both looked at each other. There was a pin drop silence for a while. "Call Saurabh here, Avantika," said Karan. Meanwhile, Varun called Pallavi.

All of them were together in a short while. Karan started talking, "We are losing our trust. The market share is on a decline. I think we should together go and talk to dad."

There was a consensus among all.

Mr. Lal was still thinking about the dream he had. Probably for the first time in his life, he felt ethereal.

To his surprise, all his children entered the room. The pious vibrations around him vanished. He gave them an arid look and prepared himself for the confrontation.

"Dad," Karan said, "the shareholders and management committee has decided that you should pass the power of attorney to one of us." He was not elusive at all.

They didn't ask me about my health. Mr. Lal felt really bad. They want everything without any hard work. If they leave me to die after taking everything, what would I do?" He went into a stupor on his wheelchair.

The family was again disappointed by his reaction. They called the nurse and left the room.

Chapter-4
The Ignition

"Congrats Dad! You've stepped out of the room on your own today after nine months. I've got a walking stick for you," Karan said as he walked towards Mr. Lal.

Though the corporeal appearance of Mr. Lal didn't seem to be in good state, he was feeling relaxed mentally and back to life after a long time.

Varun wanted to hold his hand, but he was disallowed.

"Oh! Dad, you are back, it's party time again. Come on, let us invite everyone and celebrate your grand comeback."

As Mr. Lal happily agreed to the proposal and the gloom over Pratibha Niwas disappeared. Everyone got busy in making arrangements for the press conference and the party.

Mr. Lal was sitting in his room and trying to force his eyelids to remain open as he was unwilling to recollect the past memories. But the agony of the last few months was indomitable. Notwithstanding his all his efforts, thoughts overwhelmed his persona and he was carried away by his recent memories. Thankfully, the nurse interrupted his thoughts to give him his medicines. He sat for his morning prayers, this was an age-old ritual. He offered his prayers in the small prayer hall of his house. Despite improved conditions there remained a sense of discontentment in him that lurked somewhere. He feared to reinstate himself in the corporate world successfully. He rehearsed for the press conference in front of a mirror for the first time in his life. The confidence which he used to exhibit was unseen. He again suffered the pangs of the past.

After a long period of gloom, Pratibha Niwas was bright with glittering with lights again. Everyone was cheering except.........

"Karan, are you happy? Dad is again joining the business again," Latika whispered in his ears.

"Latika, we all tried to prove ourselves but the trust and goodwill Dad carried in the corporate world is unattainable and out of reach. So, for the business, it is good that he is coming back. But this time I will try to take up more responsibilities from him. Others have the same opinion as well. Everyone was overly excited and merry about the grand welcome party but...

Mr Lal came out of his room and saw everyone running around making arrangements for the press conference that to take place in the evening. His mind took him way back to the golden years of his reign. His imaginations flew over the earlier days when he used to flaunt his charisma effectively and impressively. He could retrospect amid applause all around. His morale was boosted and he regained the confidence to address the conference.

That's the shape of life. It is highly elusive, one moment it is pathetic and another moment it is joie de vivre.

However, the media people started coming at the appointed time. Everyone seemed to be enthusiastic to welcome the legend. Needless to say, they were more interested to express solicitude to Mr. Lal.

Mr. Lal anxiously entered the hall. All eyes were staring at him making him feel more conscious and a bit nervous too at the same time. The feebleness in his physique was evident and his charisma was badly smitten by his illness. There were whispers all around.

"Is it his welcome party or his farewell?"

"Will he be able to prove himself again?"

"He should announce his representative now."

"It is his age to relax now."

"To whom do you think will he would hand over the responsibilities?"

"Who you think is more capable, Karan or Varun?"

These whispers were enough for Mr. Lal to falter, get irritated and restless. He viewed all this as a prelude to something scarier. "Why are these people worried about to whom we would hand over my reigns? That's my discretion and prerogative!" He felt reluctant to stay there anymore but he restrained his emotions and took his seat.

Karan got a chance to speak, "My dad has given his golden years to this business world. The slow economic growth in our country cannot discredit his efforts. He is back to work, though not in his original form he would soon regain it. Let's welcome him back."

There was a huge applause. The sound of claps which enthralled him once seemed like a thunderstorm now. He was dispirited and did not wish to handle the mike owing to his hidden fear. Everyone expected him to talk but he said "Sorry" and expressed his wish to go back to his room to rest.

Karan announced, regretting his father's inability to address the gathering, "Please enjoy the sumptuous dishes arranged for you at the party."

Some media personnel wanted to interview Mr Lal but he refused politely and went back to his room. He himself was surprised at his unusual behaviour. Amazingly, he was not amused by this swanky lifestyle contrary to his earlier attitude. He sat on his bed with his eyes closed and, in a jiffy, his entire past reeled out in his mind- three decades of fame and a few months of pain: that's what his life had been. Now what? His mind was full of thoughts. He lied down flat and after a long struggle, slipped into the arms of sleep.

***

He saw himself sitting near a pond of fresh sparkling water. The beauty of nature behind the pond was marvellous. He wanted to quench his thirst as he was feeling more thirsty than ever before. He was just a few steps away from the pond. As he moved forward to put his hands in the water, he realized that he was glued to a beautifully carved carpet on which he was sitting. He tried hard to leave the carpet but in vain. Looking up, he saw an elderly lady in dirty clothes standing nearby. She was about to push him…

***

"Sir…..Sir… it is time for supper," a voice woke him. It was the nurse who took the dinner trolley from the servant and asked Mr. Lal to freshen up. He, like an obedient child, followed the instructions and had his dinner before going to sleep.

He got up early the next morning, took his walking stick and went out of the house for a stroll. The morning seemed fresh and healthy. As usual, he chanted his morning prayers but his mind was with full of disturbed thoughts. "Please move to a side sir," a voice touched his ears. He turned around to look back where he found a street-sweeper standing on the side with a heap of dirt collected. The sweeper again repeated, "Please be on one side, sir, I have to clean the place."

"Oh! Sorry……..I am very sorry… and ……… thanks."

He felt like a shower of joy in his mind. "I think she is right. I am moving with a burden of my past. I should be on one side now. The side that would fulfill me. Enough of years have gone in vain. Now I must look for and work towards building the principles and ideology that infuse peace in relationships. But real peace is somewhere else. I should go towards the true and meaningful relationships. He was calm, relaxed, and felt detached from the world. It was at this moment, that he could visualize the transparent self.

Chapter-5
The Surrender

Mr. Lal went back to his room. He could see the morning scene from his window. Each moment the sun became even brighter. He thoroughly enjoyed this increasing brightness. He realized that his conscious watching of a morning scene made him feel excited and truly happy. He enjoyed all the moments of the present when his mind was free from his past. Being happy is not *that* difficult, he thought. He enjoyed his morning chores and after breakfast, he again went out to enjoy the peace of Mother Nature. He walked on and on without realizing that he had left his house miles away. He felt tired and so stopped to lie on a bench in a park. He relaxed there for some time. His mind did not permit him to go back to his house. He decided in favour of his mind and checked the amount of cash he was carrying. He had 2500 rupees. He hired an auto rickshaw and went to the railway station.

There he sat on a train and felt the kind of freedom that the bird feels when it leaves its golden cage for a limitless sky. It was a different kind of experience altogether. He had no grudge of the past, no worry of the future. His mind transcended in the flow of time. He went off to sleep. The train stopped at many stations. Although Mr. Lal did not know his destination, there was no sign of worry on his face. It was as if he had surrendered before his destiny. So, he got down at one station as per the divine wish. The aura of the place welcomed him and he felt a strange sense of inner freedom. His feet kept walking. His mindless wandering took him to a temple, where he sat on the stairs.

On the other end, Prathibha Niwas was in chaos. Where was the owner of the house? Was he abducted? Where had he gone without telling anyone? The whole family was taken aback by this sudden mishap. The media, police, hospitals all were on high alert. Mr. Lal was MISSING!! WOOH!! The family was facing trial from the media; questions were fired like bullets from the gun.

"Oh! Dad has ruined everything!" The family cursed Mr. Lal for this defamation.

Mr. Lal, on the other hand, visited a number of temples. He was cured naturally. He himself was surprised at how he was getting food and shelter. He just surrendered to divinity and everything was arranged for him. One afternoon, he felt hungry and observed that there was no "langar" that day. All of a sudden, a car stopped near him. A little girl came out with a plate full of food and handed it over to him. He was so touched by the divine grace that his belief that he was on the right path was reinforced. The divine control over his fortune filled him with gratitude.

He had grown a long beard. His clothes were dirty. It was difficult for anyone to recognize him. One day he was sitting under a tree and beautiful lyrics touched his senses.

"One who has surrendered himself to His wish need not worry for anything, as all his worries will be taken care of by Him."

He enjoyed the lyrics and music. Suddenly he had a flash of insight which demystified the hidden meanings of the strange dreams he had been having. He could easily gather that the rusty iron chain and the carved carpet were the bondages of materialism and the pious light and the pond of sparkling water were the nectar of divine love. The lady dressed in shabby clothes must be the sweeper who made him realize his divine call; he could easily realize that he himself had tied the rusty chain on his feet but had not tried to open it with his hands which were always free.

He stepped inside the temple from where the sound was coming. A saint was singing the "bhajan". He then started a story, "One day, a father asked his son to go to the market and get some eatables for him. He told him about the urgency of getting the things as he was feeling hungry. The son went to the market but on his way, he found a juggler. He stopped there to enjoy the show. A person came there to remind him of his job. But he ignored him. After a while, another person came and told him that his father was annoyed, but the son kept watching the juggler. It started getting dark and shops got closed by the time he realized that it was too late for him to buy the desired things. The son had to bear the punishments."

"What is so special about the story?" The saint continued, "Nothing special. But if you deeply think about the hidden message of the story, then think that God, as the father, send us to the world for a special purpose and we, as sons, get busy in the games shown by the Mother Nature, depicted as a juggler. The juggler keeps us busy in the illusions just like we are trapped by the pleasures of the world. We tend to forget our real job. Then the difficulties in the form of messengers come to remind us about our real job. As the difficulties are over, we forget the messages. Then it is the time for old age to alert us about our true work. At last, the dawn of death appears and there is no time left for us to enjoy the divine pleasure. Till the time adversities hit us, we pray for the divine intervention but as we are out of the unfavourable circumstances, we tend to indulge in worldly pleasures. These worldly attachments seeming so lustrous to us and they keep on inviting us repeatedly making us believe the unreal as real."

The saint left many unanswered queries in Mr. Lal's mind.

So I have been living in an unreal world. How real is this feeling? If only I could find someone who would help me sail from darkness to light; if only I could get a mentor, a guide to show me the real path of peace. There was a true yearning to reorient himself with the help of an enlightened person. It was actually the sign of true surrender and as if divinity was prescient about its happening in his life. He slowly walked down the stairs with thoughts of searching for a true transformer. While walking on the street with elated feelings, he suddenly stamped on a pot that was on a mat...Smash! Water poured out of the pot, and he realized that he had walked over the mat without paying attention to the pot. He looked at the young woman in her early 30's who was meditating on the side of the mat.

"Oh! Please accept my apologies," Mr. Lal said in a humble voice. The lady got up and cleaned the place.

Chapter- 6

The beginning of a spiritual journey

It was dusk by then. Stars had started appearing on the sky. The voice of psalms and the music of bells ringing in the temples made the environment pious.

"…………I really apologize," Mr. Lal said again as the lady got up.

Mr. Lal was so touched by the mesmerizing aura of the young woman that he kept looking at her. Suddenly, he fell on the mat and started weeping. She came and sat near him and looked at him tenderly. After a few moments, he opened his eyes and looked at the woman again.

She was clad in a saffron-coloured saree that had a white border. Her long black hair was neatly tied up. Her face had a special touch of morning beauty. Her glowing forehead spoke about the simplicity within. The divinity itself sprinkled around her.

The mystique on the girl's face made Mr. Lal more inquisitive about her.

"Who are you……..?" he uttered.

"Sadhika Sakshi," the woman replied.

"I am confused. How do I address you? You are endowed with a special charm that is so mesmeric."

"That's your gratefulness, Mahashaya," she smiled and replied.

"I am a desperate seeker. This name is given to me by Gayatri Ma. She says Sakshi means witness. That means I am the witness of my own karmas, a witness of all happenings around me. I am not a doer. You too appear to be a seeker. We all are privileged souls having a single father. You can call me your sister." Her enthralling words were spoken with deep humbleness.

"Mahashaya, Mahashaya......... Is everything fine?" She broke the silence.

"I need a mentor. Please help me." The yearning was evident on his face.

Sadhika Sakshi smiled and said, "Come with me." She packed her stuff and started walking.

Mr. Lal thoughtlessly walked behind her. It was as if his reflexes were conditioned to be effortless and his brain worked on natural instincts.

They entered a beautiful hermitage. The dim lights but the positive vibrations of the place touched his heart. Sadhika Sakshi told someone to arrange for necessary things. Soon, arrangements were done for his bath and food. While eating he realized he was feeling famished.

He stayed in a simple cottage with another. To his surprise, the man was not speaking at all. He wanted to share the alterations his life was going through, but the man was not interested in talking. Anything that Mr. Lal asked him, he just smiled and did not reply.

"What a strange attitude he has." Mr. Lal thought. Then he turned his face to the other side and slept. It was the most comfortable sound sleep he had ever had. Next morning was even more beautiful. As he looked out of the cottage, his eyes cherished the peaceful aura of the Ashram. The beautiful lawn was inviting him to talk. There were many people moving around and busy with their daily chores, but one strange thing which was disturbing him was the silence of the place.

"How strange! So many people around but none of them are speaking."

"Mahashaya!" A melodious voice interrupted his thoughts. That was Sadhika Sakshi. "Please get ready. Gayatri Ma will meet you after two hours. Sadhak Naman will take you to her. I hope Sadhak Bodhi helped you last night."

"Who is that?" he asked.

"He shared the room with you and if Gayatri Ma permits you to stay here, you'll have to stay with him in the same cottage."

"Oh! But he doesn't speak."

Sadhika Sakshi smiled and said, "Please be there on time."

Mr. Lal was ready much before the scheduled time. He wished someone would talk as he felt very lonely. He actually felt disgruntled at the attitude of people around him. There was a farrago of thoughts in his mind. Those few moments were enough for his distorted past to overpower his positive strength. He was confused about "What next." He had been wandering for the last 6 months and he was missing his own people for the first time. There was no one to talk. The silence of the place was forcing him to eschew his meeting.

"Let's go," Naman had come to take him along. Mr. Lal had waited for this meeting for long but at that point in time, his zeal was gone. Disheartened, he followed Naman.

The hermitage was truly beautiful. He could even listen to the voice of a water spring nearby. "This silence is peaceful too," he thought while walking.

What a unique power of our mind to reinforce us in either direction. Positive, negative; creative, destructive; good, bad. The human mind can easily be conditioned to anything. We reinforce it or we get reinforced by it; is a matter of our choice. Amazing are the ways of God to leave us to choose at will.

Mr. Lal's mind oscillated between the choices he had. They reached the cottage. Sadhak Naman showed him the way and stood behind him.

He knocked on the door.

"Who is it?"

"Me. Rajit."

"Why do you want to meet me?"

"I am searching for real peace."

"Come."

He walked in.

The small neat cottage was full of peace. A lady in her mid-fifties was sitting on the single cot.

"Take that stool," she pointed to a stool that in a corner.

He took the stool and sat on it.

"This path is really tough. It needs lots of patience, forbearance and you need to be grateful even when you are tested. Would you be able to abandon the worldly pleasures?"

He was thinking that she was younger to him so what should he call her?

Gayatri Ma read his confusion. "Drop your age. Your confusion will get sorted."

"Ma," the word was spontaneous, "I kept running behind wealth but now I feel I squandered by my own children. They need my wealth, not me."

"Son, you are a businessman. You might understand the dialect of profit and loss. The gain of respect in the material world moved you away from the spiritual wealth but the loss of respect lead you towards spiritual gain. Almost 30 years of respect and 9 months of disrespect - What is more profitable in terms of your spiritual growth? Understand your divine call. Don't you think these are the divine ways that allow detachments for our spiritual growth?"

There was a pause for a while. Mr. Lal felt like he had been released from the heaviness on his heart. He was speechless.

After a few moments, he gathered himself enough to speak. "Please allow me to be your disciple," the doyen was in his most polite mode.

"Rethink, this is the most difficult path."

"Give me a chance."

"Take your time. Stay for 3 months and then decide. The life of a seeker is a bed of thorns."

Hesitatingly, he asked, "Why don't people communicate here?"

"They do." Gayatri Ma smiled and said, "You will get the answer soon."

Chapter-7
The life of a seeker

"You will be called as Satyatma from now onwards," Gayatri Ma declared.

"What"? Mr. Lal swallowed his angst within.

"A true seeker needs to learn to be detached to his name. Go and understand the job assigned to you, Sadhak Satyatma," saying this she ended the conversation.

Thousands of thoughts rabbled in his mind. "Drop my name! It took me years to flounder it." He walked back to his cottage in a dazed state.

"Can you cook?" Sadhak Naman asked as he was walking along with him.

Mr Lal was surprised.

"Gayatri Ma told me to ask what kind of job you would like to do. All the seekers need to take some duty and responsibility. Do you know how to cook?"

"No."

"Do you know how to milk the cows?"

"No."

Mr. Lal realized his dependency on the servants. Life had been so kind to him that he was served everything before he asked.

"Can you water the plants?"

"Oh! Yes." At last, he had a job.

"Your duty hours will be 1 hour every morning and evening."

"Fine," Satyatma went to his cottage. He saw Bodhi cleaning the corridor.

The first meeting with a mentor was undoubtedly sprightly but he was not able to ensconce himself with the place. The whole day he couldn't find anyone to communicate. At night he told Bodhi that he didn't have an alarm clock to get up early in the morning.

Bodhi just smiled and crept in the laps of darkness.

Obviously, everything was strange for Satyatma. There was not a single trace of sleep in his eyes.

"What am I doing here? Without my name, without my bed!"

Suddenly he had a flashback, "Stay here for 3 months and then decide. The life of a seeker is a bed of thorns." There was a break in his thoughts.

The morning bells were ringing. Satyatma got up and after he was through with his daily chores, went to the garden to water the plants.

Unwillingly, he did all the routine jobs of a gardener.

As the clock struck 7, he felt relieved. It is the human nature if you are sitting in a room and you bolt it from inside then the sense of bondage is not there but if someone latches it from outside then you don't feel free. There will always be a difference in the attitude of a person when he himself chooses something at will or he is forced to choose. He was facing the same problem. It was becoming difficult for him to manage the conflicts he was facing. He would do his duty with a sense of bondage inside.

"It's been 2 months and I don't see any progress in my quest for realization," Satyatma found himself in a wary state of mind. There is no one with whom I can relate to here. He was trying to comprehend his circumstances.

"SATYATMA..........." A rebuking voice shattered his thoughts. He rushed out. Gayatri Ma was standing near the garden. He was delighted to see his mentor again after a long time.

"Ma, I am so happy. You called me?"

"Satyatma, you are not doing your duties properly. You were given the responsibility to take care of the garden. Half the plants are not in a good state. It was your duty to take care of the plants just like your own kids."

"But Ma! I've been assigned morning and evening duty & I do my duty religiously."

"Half the plants have reached the death stage. You do your duty without realizing that each plant needs special care. You have made yourself time bound. A responsibility, if sees time, is not fulfilled in actual terms. Time is just a measure of discipline in our life. But duty is worship. Build a relationship with your duty. Just like you feel responsible towards your relationships, take responsibility for your duty also. Work, duty, and responsibility should not be time bound. Did you ever try to make a time-bound program for your special clients in your business? Any job assigned to you; even if it is meagre to define should be taken as magnificent. Perform your work like no one else can do it. That should be related to your courage to finish it, not to the time frame. Only then you will be able to do justice with your calibre and with your duty too. Work done as per time limit is not meant to be completed. It is only when it speaks about the calibre, courage, and commitment of the person who performs it. The 3 C's define the 4th C i.e. the character of the person who performs the job. His character is not defined by his outer looks but by his outlook towards his work and responsibilities."

He could not stop thinking. "Thousands of rebukes I have given to my employees but the kind of teachings Gayatri Ma has given is tremendous. I feel a meld of sweetness and purity of thoughts. I am feeling like a shirker. She has shown me the right path. Any work assigned to me is my special client. I will entertain my special client with great efforts.

The next morning the flowers chirped about the special gardener treating them.

Chapter-8
The True Acceptance

Sadhika Sakshi entered the cottage. "How are you, Mahashaya?"

Satyatma was trying to meditate, but his thoughts were rebelling. When her melodious voice attracted his senses, he turned his face to Sadhika Sakshi.

"Come, Young Girl, please take a seat." He made a place for her to sit.

"It is over two months now. Have you found some peace or are you still wandering in its search?" she asked.

His face paled. "I really can't say. I am so confused. Gayatri Ma does not give me time to learn about "BRAHM." I want the supreme knowledge so that I can leave the miseries. I feel miserable I want to be on the real path of knowledge."

"Wait for the right time. Ma wants you to learn how to mortify your ego first. So, she is not giving you the time to learn about the divine path of truth. How can she pour the pure nectar in a dirty vessel? A raw slate is better than a scribbled one. Your mind has so much scribbled on it. Drop the confusions, the past, and then go to her. You need to accept your circumstances wholeheartedly. Erase all the scribbles and be plane. Live your present, completely leaving aside the past and the future. Your past is the dust and the future is to be reaped by the present. Don't use the dust as an ingredient to make the fresh food. Clean the dust around you and feel light. The heaviness inside you is the biggest obstacle on your way to divine truth."

...............Silence.

With a simple smile, Sadhvi Sakshi looked at the varied expressions on Satyatma's face for some moments. Then she left the pensive Satyatma.

Satyatma was perceptive to himself. It was actually the right time to enter into the periphery of his mind. The peonies of his thoughts started dancing in his mind. His perfidious and diligent thoughts lead him to make a serious expedition within.

"Am I holding my past? Am I not accepting my present?

The dark night of my past

Is so dark that I am not able to see through it.

The bright light of my future is so bright; that I am not able to walk through it.

This present moment is so complete, so fulfilled; that I can live my life through it.

Ah! The agony of past can perish.

Who has seen the future to relish?

The present moment is the only moment to cherish.

To live, to be content and to admire myself, the real 'ME'."

All delusions eloped. Satyatma felt light. What an immense power one's mind has! One's mind can change a person forever. The dimensions of a mind can't be ascertained. If it works in a positive direction, a person can create wonders but if it gets diverted in a wrong direction; a person can torment himself and the society. His thoughts moved freely within him and there were no strings attached to the time periods of any sort.

He went out of his cottage and quietly sat on the lawn. He tried to accentuate the lyrics of a bhajan coming from some distance.

"I didn't leave my anger, my rage.

I didn't leave the unreal.

Then why did I leave the real Me?

I took immense care of my material things.

Those material things are just like lustrous stones.

Then why did I leave the real diamond?"

While enjoying the lyrics he went back to his cottage. His eyes got moist, tears started flowing, it was like the pain from his heart flowed from his eyes. For the next few moments, he wept sitting on the floor with folded hands. Then he felt calm, peaceful, and fulfilled. His tears washed all his doubts about the present situation away.

"You cried for him today. You are on the way to truth. Drop all your worries and move ahead. The nectar of bliss is waiting for you," Bodhi spoke for the first time.

A calm smile appeared on his face and lit his forehead. For the first time, he did not feel any urge to speak. Silence, that annoyed him a few days back, was finally enjoyable. He understood that when you talk to yourself, you don't want to interact with anyone. If you can interact with yourself you never feel lonely or bored. When you don't feel lonely or bored, you always enjoy.

Satyatma enjoyed the freedom from speaking, it was as if he was celebrating this supreme freedom. Almighty's nectar of bliss is all pervasive and no place is away from him. As he is everywhere, the whole universe is blissful. How amazing it is that we all stay in the vast ocean of bliss, yet we still we thirst for it. Those moments filled him with gratitude. It became easy for him to accept his surroundings.

It was the true beginning of his quest. Learning the art of acceptance was the stepping stone of his spiritual journey. No one can progress in any field until the time things are not accepted the way they are. This art of acceptance is not easy to understand. Only a strong person can accept things wholeheartedly. It is not possible till the time we are not aware of the fact that to change our circumstances, we need to change our perception. Things do not synchronize with our expectations just as we are not as we are expected to be.

A natural happiness penetrated in him showing him the right path. He embraced his life as it was coming to him. Why worry? What to complain? He couldn't stop telling himself that the day was truly fruitful. He felt contented. He had no worry of past or future.

He closed his eyes. He wanted to realize that moment completely. For a couple of seconds, he felt timeless, ageless, free of miseries. With immense gratitude, he slept in peace.

Chapter-9

A new Dawn

"An old woman was walking on a road with a heavy bundle of clothes in her hands. A horse rider passed her. When she saw that horse rider, she requested him to carry her bundle for some distance. He refused. As he went ahead he thought what if the bundle had valuables in it, he could have easily eloped with it. The same thought flashed through the old woman's mind at the same moment. "Thank God," she thought.

The horse rider turned back and asked her to hand over the stuff. She replied, "Thanks for your concern. But now I will carry my bundle myself. One who resides in each one of us has already narrated your idea of running away with it."

A Swamiji was giving sermons to a small gathering. He was talking about miraculous vibrations. The story he narrated left a clear impact on Satyatma's mind. Do vibrations actually work? Does positive energy exist? How can we possess these energies? Endless queries danced in his mind. "Ah! What if Gayatri Ma calls me today?" he thought. He felt a touch on his shoulder. "Gayatri Ma wants to meet you," a voice cracked in his ears. He turned around, stunned. "What?"

"Gayatri Ma is calling you. She asked me to call you," saying this, the person went on his way.

Is this a coincidence or something else, he wondered. He stood overwrought for a few seconds outside her cottage. With his heart skipping beats, he stepped inside.

"Welcome Satyatma. Please sit down."

"Ma, you called me after so long!"

"Is it? You were not ready for the meeting till now, son"

"I was desperate to meet you. I think I was ready for it."

"You think, you were. In this world, things don't happen the way we want. They just happen. We are the part of the happenings around us. When we accept the happenings, we start responding. Otherwise, we keep reprimanding the situations. Although you've now accepted your surroundings, your vibrations still hook to your negative stride. Let me explain why I call you after so long through a story."

After a while, she started telling the story.

"There once was a prophet who received an invitation from a king to stay at his place. He accepted it and stayed for a month at the king's palace. One fine evening the prophet saw a piece of gold jewellery in a bathroom. He took it and eloped. After a while, the king and his men started searching for the jewel.

The prophet was naturally blamed for the act. After 3 days he came back and returned the jewellery. The king asked him why did he return. "Your Majesty, I stayed at your palace for a month. I ate whatever was made by your cook. Please check if you've changed your cook." The king ordered to do so. The main cook had gone on a holiday. So another cook was working temporarily. The cook on temporary duty was called and was asked about his earlier profession. He told everyone that he was a thief earlier but now he wanted to reform himself.

The prophet said "My Lord, I am really sorry to commit this heinous act of stealing. The negative vibrations of your cook and the meals of "rajsik" nature filled my mind with the dirty thoughts of stealing. After stealing, I ran to the forest where I ate some fruits and suffered from diarrhoea. That led to detoxifying and cleansing of my system. Eating food of "satvik" nature purified my mind and I realized my mistake. This mind is like a double-edged sword. It can channelize the negativities and the positivities. We just need to be cautious about it. After purification, I am now back to my own self. Please allow me to go back to my fort of self-possession."

Satyatma felt a fillip to his thoughts again. Vibrations do work miraculously.

Gayatri Ma continued, "Satyatma, it has been approximately three months that you have been staying here. You've been eating the "satvik" meals. You are surrounded with pious souls. Your inner self-needed time for cleansing. Actually, our body and mind are made by the ingredients taken from Mother Nature. The Mother Nature is highly illusive and so poses the circumstances in such a manner that we are trapped in it. So it becomes necessary for us to create a bulwark of self-control and self-discipline to keep us disillusioned. This is difficult but constant practice and awareness can make it possible. Now that you've been detoxified, it is the time to purify your inner self. This will help you to acclaim your inner beauty. For this, you need to follow the right discipline for your mind and body."

The dulcet dialogues of the mentor penetrated his mind and he felt a sense of pure freedom. He asked, "What is the right discipline, Ma?"

"Discipline is not bound by anything. We can learn right discipline from a liquid. A liquid changes its shape as per its vessel. When it spills it can reach anywhere. When it follows its discipline, it helps; but when it is out of discipline, it goes awry. We, as human beings, should be disciplined in order to keep our body and mind free from being diseased. We can be at ease if we follow the right way to live. A truly disciplined person realizes the true freedom: that is the freedom from miseries."

One thing was pellucid in Satyatma's mind that whatever happens happens for good and is pre-decided by God. Our short-sightedness is far behind his unconditional love for us.

Satyatma felt eternal blessing. He was overwhelmed with the idea of learning the art of living. It was time for Gayatri Ma's meditation. With high esteem for Gayatri Ma in his eyes, he went to his cottage.

Life is simple but we complicate it by not understanding the art of living. We spend our lifetime proving "what I am" instead of analyzing "who I am." Strange are the ways of the living. We believe the unreal to be real and see the real as unreal. What a paradox! We make rules of virtues and then pander to break our own rules. We cling to the inappropriate ways of indiscipline and leave aside self-discipline. We tend to blame others instead of blaming our own self, which is not possessed by us.

There was a clear strife between the materialistic and spiritual strides of life. Finally, there was a directing force that was helping Satyatma to move towards his ultimate goal.

Chapter-10

The Spiritual Management

Things that were abstruse were becoming lucid. Satyatma's eyes showed clear exuberance. That was probably the liveliness of his spirit. Spiritual tendencies can transform a materialistic person into his real form. The eternal beauty which remained covered by the outer shell had found its way. Satyatma had truly started admiring the eternal self. He started following the right discipline and the grace of his face clearly showed his determination.

"Oh! My dear soul! My bundle of clay,

You'll move on one day.

You'll move on one day.

You had told yourself that you will gain spiritual heights during this birth.

But you again bent to the illusionary nature of circumstances and give up.

You have taken so many births but

You don't understand that

You'll move on one day.

You 'll move on one day."

A melodious voice enchanted Satyatma's senses. In his endeavour as a seeker, he entered a small hall from which the voice was coming. There, in the hall, was the illuminated aura of none other than his mentor, Gayatri Ma. She was giving a spiritual discourse to the people who had come to the hermitage to meet her. Satyatma sat in a corner.

After singing the bhajan, she started:

"The human life is the most privileged one amongst all the lives. God blessed us with the freedom to act but has kept the advisory role to himself. He does not interfere in whatever we want to do but suggests the right way. By doing so, he indicates how to manage our spirituality. He wants us to move on to the next level of spirituality after passing through the tests of the previous level.

Just as a student gets promoted to the higher class after clearing the exams of the previous class, a complete lifetime is given to us with many testing episodes. Each testing episode gives us a chance to increase the fertility of our mind. If we pass with flying colours, we reach the next level. If we fail, it gives us a lesson but we are not demoted till the time we accept the suggestions of God given to us during this lifetime. Just as we cover ourselves with a blanket when we sleep, establish the same faith that we are covered by God all the time. With such faith, no testing episode can shake us. Learning from our failures and passing our tests makes this lifetime a spiritual journey. Our waking consciousness leads to insights leading to purification of our inner self. Constant and continuous practice is the key to maintain outpace on our spiritual journey. There are three ways which help us reach our destination are:

The Path of knowledge

The Path of karma

The Path of surrender.

People who profess the path of knowledge believe in logic and details of spirituality. They need proof for their beliefs.

People who follow the path of karma believe that their good deeds can help them to reach spiritual heights.

The followers of the path of surrender believe that complete faith and love for God is the only way to the ultimate unity.

Follow any religion, belong to any caste, creed, or culture, but getting a human body is the only prerequisite to walking on the spiritual path. It is only a human prerogative to reach the spiritual heights. You need to ascertain, determine, and realize your goal which is to establish communion with God and then stay connected. It is not a one time job. A true seeker must diligently keep practising the spiritual management. Just as other things in the material world are learnt through management, which includes proper planning, organizing, staffing, directing, and controlling, spirituality also needs to be managed. Spiritual management can then help us to manage other spheres of life properly. Any doubt?"

Many inquisitive faces looked at Gayatri Ma.

"Ma?" someone stood up, "we are given relationships at home, at workplace, and at times some unrelated persons like politics etc. disturb us. How can we be spiritual all the time?"

She had a subtle smile and said, "Spirituality is the most misunderstood concept, son. God gifted us this human body along with our relationships. Just as we accept all the relationships given to us, we need to accept our relationship with him. As he gave us birth, he is our true relative and will always be. Spirituality means belonging to your own spirit, our own self. Material relationships are given to us to realize our truly unaffected self. The testing episodes of our life are the times when we are affected only distorted love of our loved ones. Passing these tests is possible through spiritual management. If you are spiritually strong, no politics can affect you."

"But Ma, how can we leave other work and start with spiritual management?"

"Being spiritual means staying in your true spirit. Don't consider it as a job. O.K., tell me, when you leave for your workplace, do you take your family members along?"

"No."

"Why not?"

"I need to pay attention to my work."

"What if your family members face a problem and need you during your working hours?"

"Then I'll leave all my work and go to my family."

"So you prioritize your responsibilities."

"Everybody does."

"That means you keep your relationships in your mind even when you are at your workplace."

"I think, yes."

"When you face any kind of financial, physical, or emotional problems you feel your relationships by your side."

"Yes."

"What do you do to show your loved ones that you care for them?"

"I balance my work with my relationships by spending time with them."

"One who blessed you with all riches of the possession of your body and human life, with whom you have an eternal relationship, what do you think, spending a few moments with him or offering your material oblations are good enough to show your love for him? What will happen if you show a candle to the Sun? His boundary-less, limitless unconditional love is beyond your imagination. Even a single drop of qualm can spoil the taste of spirituality in your life. Anything in this world is the matter of matter. Matter exists in 3 forms - solid, liquid, and gas. If you become solid, you cannot change. The best way to live in this world is to be like liquid. Change and accept things just as liquid. But to achieve spiritual heights, be like gas: just flow everywhere. So... flout, float, or flow, you decide. Perform your duties, but always be attentive to your origin. Your response to your origin should be elastic and this elasticity is learnt as you progress on the divine path. It also keeps us attentive. To err is human. The attentiveness to the origin reduces the frequency of mistakes and helps us to flow in divine grace. But this needs constant practice."

The dialogues were full of insights. Satyatma was immovable.

Chapter-11

Ego-The Little Demon

There was a fresh fresco in making in Satyatma's heart. His mind and body seemed fresh as never before, the 68-year-old legend was rejuvenated. That day, Satyatma had opted to go to the market to buy some essentials for the kitchen. Sadhak Naman accompanied him. They left during the morning hours. On their way to market, he asked Naman how he had entered the path of spirituality. Naman told him that the circumstances had forced him to commit suicide but Sadhika Sakshi had stopped him. She told him to assume that he was dead and then to be reborn in the form of a spirit.

"How did Sadhika Sakshi adopt this path?"

"She was abandoned by her parents as she was born as a girl. Gayatri Ma adopted her as her own child. This hermitage belongs to Gayatri Ma's father. He was a great saint."

They reached the market. Satyatma enquired about vegetable prices. Before the vendor could reply, they saw chaos in the market. Everybody rushed to see a fight.

One of them passed a sarcastic remark, "Do you think you are Rajit Lal? Even he was not spared by God. Keep your might to yourself. Don't show it to others."

"You see your position. I am the 'Rajit Lal' of this place."

"Soon you will learn a good lesson. When he teaches a lesson no 'Rajit Lal' can stand in front of him."

The remarks left a dent in Satyatma's heart.

When they returned, Satyatma was apprehensive about whatever had happened in the market. The fight scene was fresh in his mind even after four days. He was seen as a lout and his abstinence became the reason for his next meeting with his mentor.

"You seem to be disturbed," Gayatri Ma said as he entered her cottage.

With a heavy heart he looked up, "Ma, I am feeling quite low. People think I am arrogant. They think whatever happened to me happened to set me right."

"Mr. Rajit Lal, so you are still stuck with this name."

Mr. Lal was stunned to hear this from Gayatri Ma.

"You.....You know that I am Rajit Lal?"

She smiled and replied, "I want you to be detached and the first step to detachment starts with leaving your name. Those people were talking about a name which was given to your body. We accept our name as our own until a little demon clings around us, which we call as ego. It is your ego which is looking for a defensive pergola so you can defend your name from abuses. But if you drop your name, nothing can disturb you. It is this little demon-ego which does not allow us to drop our names. Be it good or bad, it wants to be credited. It also gets hurt often as it is small and sensitive, like a kid. But by mortifying it repeatedly, we can actually get rid of it. Let it get hurt, it will not grow big. If we become attentive to the fact that whenever we listen to our ego, we indulge in a materialistic world and when we defend our ego, it grows. When this happens, it will not allow you to leave it. However, without leaving your ego you can't adopt the spiritual path as it needs complete surrender. Let me tell you a small story:

During Shivaji's reign, the people of his kingdom were really enjoying their lives. Shivaji was struck by this little demon, his ego. He started thinking that it was because of him that the people in his kingdom were wealthy, prosperous, and mighty. True masters cannot have such an attitude. So, Guru Ramdas planned to visit his disciple, Shivaji. Shiva was thrilled to see Gurudev at his palace. Guru Ramdas asked Shiva to accompany him. They left the palace immediately. They walked and almost reached the borderline of the kingdom. It was a forest. Shiva was unable to understand what his Guru wanted. At last, they stopped near a rock. Gurudev picked up a big stone and broke it into pieces. There were thousands of insects in that stone. Guru Ramdas showed it to Shiva. Looking at his confused expression, the mentor smiled and asked, "Shiva, is this forest a part of your kingdom?"

"Yes," he humbly replied.

"Were you aware of these creatures staying in the stones?"

"No, Gurudev."

"Do you think you are the one who is looking after these creatures without knowing that they were staying here?"

Shiva understood the hidden meaning of his great master. He looked ashamed of his attitude.

A true mentor always helps his disciple to learn the right ways. So he said, "Shiva, one who is omnipresent, that supernatural existence arranges for the nourishment of an unborn child in his mother's womb. Also, the mother who is oblivious about the sex and fate of her child forms a bond with the unborn without knowing about who is taking care of the growth and development of her child. Just think, one who can arrange for an unborn child and can take care of endless creatures on the Earth won't be able to look after his people staying in your kingdom? You are just a medium, a transmission channel arranged by God to serve his people."

A few minutes later Gayatri Ma again spoke, "Satyatma, till the time we think we are the employer and that we employ people to work for us; we cling to the little demon around us. But when we realize that he is the employer and all of us are employees doing the jobs assigned by him, our ego reduces. We are positioned in the right place as per our karmic order. However, we need to perform our work as per our own convictions. He only plays the advisory role. We should always follow his advice and work accordingly. But if we are unable to understand his advice then we should surrender before him. We need to gain knowledge and perform good deeds with great comfort and ease. Just like a small child who is pushed upwards in the air by his father but the child laughs without even a pint of tension in his mind about how he is left alone in the air. That is complete surrender as the child has full faith that his father will not let him fall and so he enjoys the joy ride. Similarly, we can also enjoy the bumpy rides of life if we surrender. Surrender starts with mortification of ego. It is not easy, but also not impossible. Try."

The scrimmage inside Satyatma's mind vanished. The trickling flow of the supreme discourse by his mentor made one decision clear in his mind and that was "I abandon my name."

The ego in my mind told my soul

"Look at me.

I am the one who drives the humans.

I am the one that constructs or destructs.

I am the most powerful without bars.

I can change the positioning of stars.

I can reach anywhere anytime.

For me, I AM the only prime.

If I wish I can turn you into ashes.

I can change the human mind in seconds."

The soul replied politely

"Oh! Dear! Don't boost yourself.

Without me, you will be in a gulf.

I granted you this house only to stay.

How can you leave this body away?

I have the privilege to leave you any day.

So, stay the way I want you to stay.

You are powerful till the intellect sleeps.

Awakening of mind will keep you at bay."

Chapter-12

The Art to Let Go

With constant spiritual practice and strong determination, Satyatma's path was filled with joyous confrontations. Approximately 8 years had passed since he had left his house and he was enjoying his rebirth as if he was just eight years old. All material things seemed trivial to him.

A bright looking person looked into the mirror and told himself, "You're ready for your cosmic flight." He had planned for his ultimate union. He had a clear vision in his mind about the beautiful voyage ahead. He was as excited as a kid in anticipation of pleasure. With firm determination, he sat in a lotus posture with closed eyes. He had prepared well for this meeting yet his inner sight was really stubborn to settle down. The acclaims, the media, his charismatic appearance, business meetings, all his riches, the sum total laid bare in front of his eyes. With a sudden shock, he opened his eyes and promised himself to stay calm. He tried too hard but the same thing happened repeatedly. He felt terrible.

Almost in tears, Satyatma rushed to Guru Ma's cottage yelling, "Ma, save me."

"What happened?"

"Ma, as you mentioned that spiritual management needs proper planning and just as we plan our normal chores we must plan our spiritual chores. But it seems as if my inner sight is unwilling to cooperate. As I try to meditate, it takes me again and again to my past life."

"That means you are still holding on to your past."

"But Ma, I have left those things far behind. I don't even bother about material pleasure anymore."

"Then let them come so you can make them go."

"But how is that possible?"

"I can see your determination to be physically energetic and to follow the basic guidelines of the cosmic journey i.e. loyalty, righteousness, empathy, etc. But this is not sufficient to control your inner sight. See, our mind can never sit idle, it needs momentum. Its energies dwell to break inertia. It is like a computer which can store endless photographs in its memory. So, when we start meditating we want our minds to settle down quietly. But due to its basic nature, it brings the clicked photographs to the surface even if we bury them. The records of our past lie in front of us as if they were never away from us. The more we suppress it, the more it becomes stubborn. We feel annoyed at it but it enjoys irritating us. But that is the nature of this mind. It is indispensable to understand the nature of our mind before getting into self-detection. Actually, this mind is created by the ingredients taken from Mother Nature and so it, again and again, goes back to its source. Mother Nature is highly illusive. The illusiveness of the material world is the easiest way to trigger our "self" to the attractions of materialism. Our mind plays the biggest role in doing so."

There was a mesmerizing silence in the room. Still, there was a vacuum which was waiting to get filled. Gayatri Ma spoke again, "Take an example of a clay pot. Till the time a mortal being gives shape to the clay, it will not move. Similar is the property of our mind and Mother Nature even. An immovable or a static thing attains dynamism when a living thing wants to convert it to something dynamic. Our mind too gains momentum due to the dynamic nature of our "self." So, it is equally important to understand the nature of our "self" or "soul." It is real and eternal never ceases to exist. It is highly dynamic to possess the power to channelize our mind to any direction. Imagine a car moving without a driver. Is it possible? Our mind is like a car which is driven by our "self." We assume it is the other way round. We believe that our mind is uncooperative when we are meditating." Your "self" possesses the capabilities of changing the pace of time by channelizing the "mind" in the desired direction. Again not an easy job, but with self-control, self-discipline and constantly doing so it can make it possible. You know King Parakshit was told that he would die in the next seven days. Within that short duration, he channelled his mind to attain communion with God and succeeded. Such is the power of our "self." The only limitation of our "self" is that it stays in a dormant state without a body and mind. Body and mind are the instruments given to the soul to achieve tremendous heights. The thundering power of "self" along with strong conviction can convert the unimaginable into reality in any sphere of life."

"But Ma," Satyatma asked, "how can I wake my consciousness to reach the immense power of my "self"?

"You know how to, Satyatma. Just think how could you create such a huge business empire? Without the strong conviction that would have been impossible. Even in unfavourable circumstances, you managed to work hard because you knew the importance of your work. Similarly, try and understand the importance of your spiritual conviction. You need to send positive affirmations to your mind about the premeditated program. When you are willing to take off on a cosmic flight, make your mind understand the importance of your powerful expedition. Sing psalms and talk directly to your beloved. Don't stop your past memories from coming to the surface. But just like you go through a photo album, let your thoughts come and finish watching them soon. When you let them go, your mind will be free. Keep deleting unnecessary thoughts and empty your mind. A truly empty mind will actually take you to the mesmerizing fullness of divine love."

With a calm smile on his face, Satyatma went back to his cottage.

He started feeling the deepest form of love for himself. The wanderers in the hermitage could easily feel the exhilaration coming from his cottage. The extolling voice in the form of psalms showed the divine grace bestowed on him. The whole ashram was overwhelmed and passed through a spectrum of timelessness. Very often people would hear:

Oh, my powerful mind; stay inundated

In boundary-less unconditional love of my beloved.

Whether in pain or in gain

Just stay inundated in his love.

Whether I get comments or compliments,

Just stay inundated in his love.

Whether ejected or selected,

Just stay inundated in his love.

Whether accolade or accommodate,

Just stay inundated in his love.

Soon, Satyatma became famous as a divine addicted saint and was renamed as "Satya Bhagat."

Chapter-13

Love- A misunderstood emotion

Sadhika Sakshi entered the cottage. Bhagat Ji was deep in his consciousness. She waited for him to come back to the material world. He opened his eyes with a gentle smile.

"Why do people fall in love, Bhagat Ji? And when they do, why do they get over it so soon?" she was a little disturbed.

"What happened, child?"

"I met a girl today who was willing to commit suicide as her marriage didn't work. I was not able to convince her so I brought her here. Gayatri Ma has gone out for some days. Can I call her here?"

"Fine."

After a few moments, a girl along with Sadhika Sakshi came inside.

Bhagat Ji looked at them lovingly and made a gesture telling them to sit. He said, "We love people around us, those who form our world. It is normal to hear phrases like "I Love you", "I cannot stay without you", "I can't think of parting from you", etc. Do these phrases actually denote love? Love flows between other relationships also i.e. between parents and children, brothers and sisters, and between friends too. But be it any relationship, we feel the emotional state of love till our needs and desires get fulfilled. Why do these feelings of love die with time? Is it a need for someone, or a habit of someone, or the temptation of living with the person which we denote as a feeling of love? Till the time that temptation is there, you love him or her. But what happens after this, when the desire to stay with that person is over? You say goodbye and again set off to find someone who can fulfil our needs and desire. But does this search end? If one relationship cannot be sustained, how can we sustain other relationships? One thing is clear, we love to love and to be loved. We tend to find love around us because seeking for love is our nature. When love is there, we feel happy. But this so-called state of "falling in love" is a kind of intoxication conceived by nature, a false high. As if nature wanted us to get trapped. It is like a drug induced in our blood which gives us a temporarily high, but it does not last permanently."

We live with a psychological principle called the "Principle of Hedonism", which states that we seek pleasure and tend to avoid pain. So, we tend to look forward to love around us, in someone's company, in our work, and in our own world. Soon we get addicted to love, which can be with a person or place or our work. When this addiction starts giving us pain, we feel that Oh! It was just an illusion of nature. We term this illusion as LOVE. But this illusion is a temporary high which is filled with sorrows attached to this false high. The sorrows we bear are expectations, conditions, boundaries, sacrifices, surrender, toleration, etc. which we bear with "The False High." When the imaginary love is gone we feel these sorrows because of the ego we have which is the sole creator of these thoughts correlated to the so-called feeling of love."

There was a supreme conscious discourse. Slowly, the number of people kept increasing in the room to hear him.

"If this is not real love, then what is? Can it be taught? Can we learn to love? Is it easy or so difficult to be in love? Love is a highly misunderstood concept. Actually, love is our own existence, our basic nature. Love is a feeling which is ingrained within us. It is the awareness that gives us the feeling of loving anything and everything that comes our way. A true feeling of love comes with complete faith and devotion. When we learn this art of loving, nothing can shake us from the permanent nature of happiness around us. But this feeling of love also starts after the false high is over and we actually taste the bitter parts.

When a child is crossing the road with his finger in his mother's hand, he has no fear of an accident because he has a deep love for his mother. But when love is not intense, distortion of fear creeps in. The fear of separation, the insecurity to lose the person we love enters our mind. The illusionary compartments made in our mind for our loved ones make us afraid of any kind of separation.

Another form of distortion is anger. We tend to get angry with our loved ones because of our expectations of them. When love is not deep-rooted, it will always expect or demand. When these expectations are not fulfilled, we tend to feel angry. We are filled with sorrows and pain because of unfulfilled expectations. How can we feel angry with a person we don't know? So anger is a form of distorted love, which is felt because of conditional love which is based on the 'Give & Take' philosophy.

Yet another form of distortion of love is the distortion of possessiveness. Love in this form becomes a burden for the person we love. When there is complete distortion, it becomes hatred. When we don't want to see a person, when we think in terms of all No's; it is hatred.

Bhagatji closed his eyes and became silent for a few moments.

Chapter-14

Way to pure Love

After a while, he opened his eyes and looked around. He could read the minds around him through their faces.

"All these distortions of love arise with the situations of *falling in love,*" he started again, "But tell me, without tasting the bitterness of false love, how can we relish the sweetness of pure love? Actually, when the state of falling in love gets over, we enter the stage of feeling pure love. It is due to these distortions of love, which when reaches the peak, we feel dispassion. At this time detachment happens. When we drop all doubts, queries, expectations, conditions, boundaries, and even the relationships, we can understand the intensity of deep-rooted love which is our existence. The art of loving is the art to understand the feeling of love in its true sense i.e. when love flows without condition, limitations and boundaries, it is complete, True, Pure.............. DIVINE.

Divine love is the only love which flows till the time it glows. When love glows, it becomes "BLISS". The eternal happiness for which we entered the world. When worldly love vanishes, spiritual love happens, and we forget all relationships. Actually, pure love knows no relationship. Can we describe our relationship with our own selves?

Our inner self cannot be separated from our outer self. Then what to name such a relationship? Let it flow unconditionally. The beautiful lines explaining the meaning of *"pyar ko pyar hi rahne do, koi naam na do."*

Look at the purity of love of spiritual masters. They are ready to pour their love unconditionally. SAI BABA said:

"When you look at me; I'll look at you."

The phrase doesn't literally mean that first we look at him and then he will look at us. This phrase is filled with so much pure love that BABA says: "There is not even a single moment when I don't look at you but until unless you look at me you won't be able to realize that I'm looking at you."

When we are filled with sorrow, guilt, or get into trouble because of our own wrong deeds, it is divine love that gives us the strength to cope up with all our problems. When we think of doing something good, it is the divine love which makes way for us.

If we learn the art of loving, we can feel ourselves bulwarked with divinity. It is the art of feeling blessed always which can make us feel the divine love. When we start feeling divine love, we tend to feel a similar yearning for Lord which we felt in false High. Then, we enter the world of imagination with the Lord. GOD being ever new, we never get tired of him and so the divine love is permanent. When we are filled with divine love, we start relishing the nectar of GOD which is unfathomable. Divine love leads to fullness after which we are left with no cravings of finding love beyond that. Divine love cannot be measured with education or qualification, but the only quality which is required is the ability to accept everything that happens as per our beloved's wishes. When everything is happening because of the beloved's wish, it is always right. Divine love has no queries, no ifs, no buts, no conditions, and no boundaries. When we learn to live life with such love, we actually learn the art of loving. It is this love that happened to Meerabai, Kabir, SAI BABA, Prahlad, Dhruva, Shabri, Arjuna, etc. It is this love that made them popular, though it is not what they wanted.

Learning to relish pure love requires being unconditional.

Once upon a time, Lord Krishna wanted to teach a lesson on divine love to Udhava, who had embarked on the path of knowledge. He sends Udhava to Brij (his birthplace). All the gopis surrounded him to ask the wellbeing of their beloved, Lord Krishna. Udhava gave sermons to them on attaining renunciation through the path of knowledge. At last, he gave a message to the gopis which was given by Lord Krishna. It stated that Lord Krishna was suffering from a severe headache, which could be cured only by the soil of his birthplace. But the condition was that whosoever gives the soil to Udhava will have to suffer in hell for some time.

To Udhava's surprise, all Gopis picked the soil and pleaded Udhava to take it. Udhava asked were they not afraid to stay in hell? Gopis smiled and told Udhava that if living in hell for some time can relieve the pain of their beloved, then that hell is sweeter than any heaven. This was an eye-opener for Udhava and he got an exemplary vision of divine love.

Undoubtedly there are many ways to attain GOD, but without LOVE all paths are incomplete. A few lines describing the beautiful love of the gopis to Lord are: "We are innocent, uneducated, and ignorant. How can we understand the difficult language of so many books, hymns, etc? How can we understand the meanings of so many rituals? All these things seem complicated to us. We can just understand the language of love which is innocent, unconditional, and beyond all relationships. What is between us and lord, only we and our Lord can understand. We cannot explain these feelings to anyone."

This is the art of Loving. It doesn't need making others understand how much love we have in our heart or how much we are surrounded by divinity. The world cannot understand the inner beauty of divine love. One story in the Bible explains the depth of divine love. Once upon a time a priest was lost on an island. He found only three men living on that isolated island. The priest had to stay there till the time any help could reach him. He thought of giving some spiritual discourse to the three men.

Priest: Do you believe in GOD?

The three men: Yes

Priest: What kind of prayers do you offer to him?

One old man: We say "We are three, you must be three. Help us."

Priest: (laughing) Oh! Is that a prayer? It is not the way we should pray to GOD.

The old man: Sir! We are ignorant people. Please tell us how to pray. We can learn a new prayer.

The priest helped them to learn prayers for GOD. One morning, a boat came and the priest left the island. Late that evening, the priest saw a black dot at a distance. The dot grew bigger and bigger and was coming closer to the boat. Then he saw, the old men he had left on the island running on the water. The priest got the boat stopped for them.

The Three old men (breathlessly): Sir; we forgot the prayers you taught us. Please tell us again.

Priest: Sure but first, please tell me how did you run on water and what saved you from drowning?

The old man: Sir, when you left, we became busy with our work. In the evening, we sat down to pray but couldn't remember what you'd told us. We stood near the sea and looked up. We told GOD that we had no boat to follow you so we will run. Rest we left to GOD. And we came running towards you. Now please tell us how to pray.

Priest (surprised): Your faith in GOD and your love for him is beyond the level of any wordings. GOD listens to you in whatever form you pray. You don't require any special words to pray.

This is divine love which is inexhaustible, and so we are never tired of it. We are lucky that we've got human bodies which can taste divine nectar. Oh! Dear Lord! Let love flow from me and let love come to me. Your wish means everything to me. Make me vulnerable to negativities. When the world respects me; it is because of your love and when the world rejects me, it is because you want me to feel your love. Oh! Your unconditional love makes me feel beautiful. Your boundary-less love makes me realize my selfishness. You are the nectar in flowers; the honey of bees; the pure love… the bliss. Let me feel you in such a manner that there remains no difference between you and me. Just Love…Love…Love."

The souls sitting around Bhagat Ji felt the divine nectar of pure love inside the cottage. There was a limitless flow of love all around.

Chapter-15
The Cosmic Flight

Satya Bhagat would stay focused inwards, even in public. His inner beauty was evident on his radiant face. The divine love would not stop flowing. The seventy-two years old saint was still yearning for the ultimate unity.

Gayatri Ma entered his cottage.

"Bhagat Ji," she addressed him, "Your awakening has been enthralling."

With no shades of qualms on his face, the revered saint made a place for Gayatri Ma to sit. With esteemed soberness, he asked, "Ma, why did you bother? You could have sent someone to call me."

"Bhagat Ji, your addiction to divinity is widespread now. People come to relish your sanctity. You have proved that consciousness can achieve tremendous heights at any age. I bow in front of you."

"Ma, please don't embarrass me. Your blissful ways led me to be ardent about my ultimate peace. I wandered for this peace only. But...."

Gayatri ma understood the craving of a true lover to meet his beloved. She smiled and said "Let the fetters be opened soon. God bless you." Saying this, she left.

The timeless saint sat to meditate. His mind was settled. His senses were quiescent. There were quivers in his body for a few moments which subdued in a few minutes. The aplomb was clear on his face. Tears flowed out of the eyes but he wiped them off.

His face radiated with divine warmth. A subtle smile was indelible on his face, making him purely divine. He was as static as divinity in the cosmos. It was as if the mural had been fixed at last.

Timelessness had broken all the bondages - physical, emotional, and material. His body, senses, and mind were free from all bondages. His soul was at its ultimate position – 'The flow position'. There was a free flow of feelings all around the cosmos. The universe seemed to be contained by the soul itself and soul seemed to be contained by God himself. The unbound penetration within the omnipresent was beyond all imagination. He who created the universe had blessed him with his nectar of bliss. Radiant joys entered each pore of his body. The melodies of Mother Nature, along with the unconditional love of God, wrapped his soul in a loving embrace. His soul danced freely in the radiations of this spectacular vision.

The experience was unbelievable and completely conscious.

Bhagat Ji opened his eyes. He could still feel the vibrations of joy in his body. "All I had wanted to know is known now." He was contented and complete. He opened the door and went for a stroll in the garden, barefoot. Mother Nature welcomed the newly born saint.

He smiled calmly. Wandering barefoot on the grass he pondered over the kindness his beloved had bestowed on him. "One who is all pervasive, omnipotent, omnipresent, real, blissful, eternal, never affected by illness, old age, immortal, our biggest well-wisher, just yet kind, most powerful, flawless, pure, and father of all mortal or immortal things is wonderful. Such a wonderful father shared his bliss with me! I feel like I am the most privileged person on the Earth." As he was thinking all this, he walked towards Gayatri Ma's cottage.

"Bhagatji, you've come to a realization of all things you wanted to know!"

"This realization is supreme, Ma."

"Now it is time of repayment."

"Anything for you, Ma! But what can I offer you?"

"Share your insight with people. You have been chosen by him to make divine calls. Let them know that he is not the cause of their sufferings, their sufferings are actually bitter fruits of their own karmic disorders. Tell them that a material life can only give them pleasure that is mixed with suffering. You can tell them that they can relish unlimited joy without even a single tinge of suffering." The pain was pellucid in his mentor's eyes as well as voice.

"I shall honour your wish, Ma."

That night, Satya Bhagat left the hermitage to fulfil a special purpose.

A bright, bald, clean shaven clad saint in white clothes was sitting under a tree and meditating. He could see complete nakedness and camouflage of Mother Nature in his supreme consciousness. People around him wondered who he was. The radiant charm on his face and the positive aura around him attracted everyone to him. Soon, there was a small gathering waiting for the saint to bless them. Satya Bhagat opened his eyes and saw people sitting around him.

"Who are you?" someone asked.

"Everything," he replied.

Confusion was apparent on everyone's face.

"I mean when I was nothing, I wanted to be something and now when I am everything, I need nothing."

"From where did you come?"

"From this world."

"Why did you come here?"

"To serve." After answering their questions, he again closed his eyes and started singing:

Oh! Almighty, everywhere.

You and you and only you.

No place is empty.

And so I am full too.

Due to you and only you.

Your unconditional love

Reminds me to love you.

You and you and only you.

People started dancing and the aura of the place changed. A person came near Bhagat Ji and said, "My name is Rehman Khan. People call me "Khan Sahib. I have a bungalow here. Can you please oblige me by accepting to stay at my place?"

Bhagat Ji smiled and said, "As he wishes."

There were whispers all around. He was the District Superintendent of Police. Why did he invite the saint to his place? The inquisitive faces were left unanswered.

Chapter-16

The interrogation

The DSP called home and instructed to make arrangements for his guest. He kept thinking as if he were planning for an interrogation. On the other hand, Satya Bhagat freely walked with him like a calm river. His smile illuminated his aura. Due to his eye-catching charisma, the DSP was not able to look straight into his eyes. The fearless saint entered his bungalow.

After supper, Satya Bhagat went into his room and sang hymns and psalms.

Knock.........knock...

"Come to DSP."

"You know that I am a DSP?"

"I even know your purpose of bringing me here."

"Oh! That means I was correct. You are Mr Lal!"

"Yes, that was the original name given to this body."

"I knew it. I wanted to call the media but something stopped me."

"His wish, son. His wish is bigger than our convictions."

"I don't believe this. If I wanted, I could easily expose you."

"O.K. Then you can call the media."

They looked at each other in the eye, but in no time the DSP's gaze was drawn to the saint's feet. He had conducted numerous interrogations during his service but he guessed this would be the most difficult one. And his guess was right.

"I am confused," he dropped his shoulders and flopped on a chair.

"Then drop your confusion."

"If you are Mr. Lal then why don't you inform your family that you are alive? Why did you disappear from your house so suddenly? Where were you till now? No one would have imagined that you would adopt this form. We looked at this as an abduction case, and the court has assumed you to be d........," he purposely swallowed the last word, "Please answer."

"His wish," the saint replied calmly, "This is the only answer to all your queries. Divine consciousness breaks all bondages and I am the blessed one."

"That is not a satisfactory answer."

"DSP Rehman Khan, before we move ahead, can I ask you a few questions?"

"Fine."

"Who are you?"

"What a strange question! Why... I am DSP Rehman Khan, you just said you know me!"

"That is the name given to your body. Do you believe this body is yours?"

Bhagatji's eyes showed his confusion.

"If this body is yours, then it would ask you before getting aged, your eyes would ask you before getting deteriorated, and your hair would have asked you before turning grey. When you have no control over your body, how can you misguide yourself by thinking that your body belongs to you? Do you have children?"

"Yes! I have two daughters and a son."

"Do they belong to you?"

Silence....

"Do you believe in the cause-effect philosophy?"

"Yes! Of course."

"If you see your body as an effect, what was the cause for your body to exist?"

"The cause is biological."

"Do you think your mother or father created you? Just indulgence of two people in a mere act of pleasure? Neither of them knows how to create a body. If they knew it, there would only be beautiful people all around. Then who created our bodies? Who decided our sex, complexion, and fate? Who created the parts of your body?"

The stunned DSP looked at him with a blank expression.

"My son, believe it or not, the supernatural existence is the only cause of our existence in this form. Our body which we think we possess is not ours. We cannot feel the eternal freedom till the time we are enslaved by our senses and keep our mind engaged in sensory pleasures only. This bondage is the result of our attachment to this body. Liberation is the inner freedom, which lies in unconditional surrender. The sense of inner freedom paves the way to ultimate detachment. Actually, we are mediums arranged by God to serve his people. We are the channel he has chosen to bring some more bodies into existence in the form of the children we think we own. But, if this body is not ours then how can the children delivered by this body be ours? We all are eternal, immortal beings but are privileged to have minds that can be directed as and when required. The thought that 'this is mine' leads to attachment and, as a result, bondage. Being aware of our privileges help in removing bondages and results in liberation. Incomplete consciousness, we realize the purpose of this body is to view it as an instrument to gain spiritual growth. The charms of Mother Nature control our body and senses. But the power of the mind is such that it breaks the illusionary trap laid by Mother Nature and helps us dance in the communion of our beloved. But this ultimate unity is only possible if divinity calls. Wait for the divine call and you will not even think for once how to leave all bondages.

"If God exists, in what form can we see him?"

"Son, God is a belief, a concept. Let us take the example of a pen. The pen would have some features. When you explain those features to a person who has never seen the pen, he will form an image of the pen in his mind. He will be able to conceptualize the image of the pen but would only believe it when he really sees it. Similarly, we also form a concept of God according to the features told to us by our holy books. But when we start meditating and try to go deep in our consciousness then with patience, practice, and endeavours you make to break all sensory bondages, your style of romancing him will change your concept into belief. With strong determination, you can change this belief into faith. It is at this time that complete surrender happens. Faith means being complete, without any qualms in your mind just embrace divinity around you. That is life. Rest is death."

"That means we should leave all our jobs for divinity. In this era of competition, how can we sustain without work?"

"Who says you need to leave your work? Inactivity is escapism. Only meditation is escapism. I am saying that make your job a part of divinity within you. Give yourself completely to your job. Be the best warrior of your work and gain esteem in whatever you do. Perform your tasks as if you are the only person chosen by him and prove that you are the best. He, as our father, expects nothing less than sky for us. He is our biggest well-wisher and wishes that we should reach the limitless heights in our work field. Make your job a passionate expedition along with spirituality. Separation from your divine love will make you corrupt in your work field. It will give birth to apathy. It is actually the divinity inside us which leads to devotion at our workplace. Taking more and more responsibilities leads to your growth. As we cannot separate our parents' name from our body, can we separate divinity from our existence? Divine love is not a job; it is your inner strength which helps in building a strong character. Without divinity, your inner strength cannot be 100% and you won't be able to perform with contentedness. To work without caring for the results is your duty. Accept all the challenges of life as opportunities. In addition, meekly giving up in face of weakness as the biggest threat.

Treat this body as a temple of divinity and utilize each second of your life by working in direction of your growth. Embrace the divine love to become more passionate in your work. That is why I said Divinity is life. Rest is death."

"But how can we embrace divinity in our work?"

"Like Arjuna. When Arjuna entered the war field, his chariot was driven by Lord Krishna. This showed that Arjuna is the "soul" who handed over his chariot depicted as his "mind or intellect" to Lord i.e. God himself. Afterwards, the Lord directed his chariot but the actual war was fought by Arjuna. Similarly, in this world of materialism, we need to hand over our mind to The Lord and let him direct us in our work. Thus we excel in whatever we do as the God is our director and we become the actors."

"One last question, please tell me your experience with God."

"Son, for that you need to be romantic with him. God has given us unique faces, even two leaves of the same tree are not similar in shape and size... everything is unique and distinguished. Then how can one person's romance be similar to the other? The divine romance of each person is distinguished and so the experience of such romance is also unique. This uniqueness of the ultimate unity can be relished by only that person who is indulged in the romance. It is immeasurable, undefined, and unbelievable; but yes! It happens in supreme consciousness. So be aware of your body and senses. Explore your uncanny capabilities and start your journey. Dance in the limitless journey of divine love. It has no end; it is boundary-less, unconditional pure love."

The night of interrogation turned to be the night of illumination for the DSP. With thorough gratefulness, he went out of the room.

Chapter-17

The Courtroom Dilemma

"Karan, can you be a little faster? We are getting late. Your brother and his darling must have reached the court already. God knows what all they have in their mind. Ugh! Why I am spoiling my mood by even thinking about them?" Latika muttered.

"Coming baby! Why are you losing your cool? Anger does not suit you, my dear. Yah! Tell me what happened?"

"What happened? You are asking me what happened. How can you forget your father's ingenuine act of throwing us with hungry wolves? I could never have imagined that they had guts to file a case over the property."

"Ha! Ha! Guts!? You clearly do not know them. They only look meek but are real creeps. I'm ashamed to call them my relatives. O.K. Now, don't increase your blood pressure for them. Let us go to our lawyer. Barrister Nirula will set them right."

The same sequence of such blame games was on at their brother Varun and sister Avantika's places.

The three kinsfolks were fighting over property distribution, the most important issue was, "Who would succeed their father in business?"

Varun and Pallavi were sitting with their lawyer, Barrister Subrato Bannerji. He appeared to be a casual man but actually was assiduous for his work. In his mid 50's, he was amongst the most well-known lawyers in the country.

Avantika and Saurabh sat outside the courtroom and waited for their turn. They seemed apprehensive. Their lawyer, Barrister

Somesh Dutt, was preparing his arguments for the hearing which was about to start.

"Come on in!" Barrister Nirula called them inside the courtroom when their turn came. Everyone followed him. The proceedings started.

"Your honour," Mr. Nirula started. "Being the eldest son, my client should be given his due. He, as per the law, stands for a chance to become the successor of his father as there is no will."

"But, Sir, my client Mr. Varun Lal has been an active partner in business along with his father. He is great at what he does and handles everything maturely."

"Objection! My lord, is my friend, Mr. Banerjee, indicating that my client is not mature to handle things properly? Excuse me, but my client, Mr. Saurabh, has given 15 invaluable years of his life to this family business. Even Mr. Lal remained munificent to him throughout."

The heated argument, along with the blame games, continued. The media, the judge, and the people all around enjoyed the melee of the family. The courtroom drama subsided with yet another "DATE" which was due next month. The family were unwilling to see each other's faces. The "Page-3" coverage the next day would highlight the murky picture of the famous family.

What a phase of life! Once upon a time, the kinsfolk who were ready to bend head over heels for each other were after each other's throats.

However, the younger generation was unaffected by the melodrama of the elders of the family.

"Saarthak, what were you doing with them?" Latika lashed out at her teen son.

"Relax, Mom, chill; you may baulk at their sight but don't tell me to do that. Keep your stuff away from us. We are childhood buddies. Don't drag us in all this. Now please excuse me," saying this the brash brat left.

Latika unloaded her frustration on her husband. Their nights were sleepless and days were stressful. There was not a single ray of hope which would give solace to the dying relationships.

How badly the worldly relations are treated at times! Speaking without realizing is just like throwing stones. Do we actually love our relations or do we just pretend to do so? Which form of love is this which forces us to uncoil the cords of blood? It is actually the paleness in our love which makes us highly insensitive?

It was again the "DATE" of another hearing in the court. The same chaos prevailed in all the three houses since morning.

"Varun," Pallavi called, "When will all this get over? I get really disturbed due to the pathetic ways of the court proceedings."

"We are left with no choice, dear. Our elders have forgotten how to behave. I don't want to be dictated every time."

The farrago of complaints was on. We land up talking more about those relationships which we are not willing to maintain and take those relations for granted which means everything to us, What an irony.

The court hearing had started.

"My Lord," Avantika's lawyer started, "These are the detailed salary slips and expenditure details of Saurabh, for your reference. These days daughters too stand for an equal and fair chance in the distribution of property."

"But Sir," Barrister Nirula interrupted, "Mr. Lal had been generous enough to gift a firm to Saurabh when Avantika got married to him."

"Yes. This man inveigled my father every time," Karan screamed.

There was a heated argument between the three lawyers.

"Order, Order. This is not your house. Please maintain the decorum of the place."

There was a pin drop silence at once. With rotten expressions on their faces, the three-kinsfolks looked at each other.

A robust man dressed in a police uniform walked into the courtroom with papers in his hands. All eyes were on him. He bowed in front of the magistrate and handed him the papers. Copies of the papers were distributed among the three lawyers.

All inquisitive faces looked in confusion.

"Your Honor, this is Mr. Lal's will."

"Who are you?"

"I am DSP Rahmaan Khan."

Chapter-18
The final verdict

The family was in disbelief and wanted to hear the complete story.

"My Lord! I am privileged to be chosen for this act by my great master, Satya Bhagatji." The DSP gratefully looked towards the door of the courtroom. Everybody turned.

The new avatar of Mr. Lal entered the courtroom. The positive aura of the enlightened saint illuminated the place. Everyone stood up and bowed towards him.

"Papa," Avantika screamed and rushed to him. Everyone else looked on without blinking.

Mr. Lal had a smooth smile on his face and his vibrant face left people spellbound. He obviously was the catalyst to solve the maelstrom in the courtroom.

"Your Honor, as you can see in the papers before you, I have transferred my material wealth equally and fairly to my worldly children as per my will."

"Mr. Lal, if you wanted to transfer the wealth, why didn't you do it before leaving the house? Why did you leave your house and what made you abandon your generous life?" the judge inquired.

"It wasn't easy, my Lord! I earned so much wealth in my life that many generations can be fed upon easily. But I became reclusive, I didn't even indulge in recreational activities. It was just a mad rush for gathering material wealth and a treacherous respect. But the nine months of painful recuperation lead me to the conclusion that material wealth is actually the cause of disorientation among relationships. I loathed worldly relationships. In that frame of mind, I decided not to give anything to my children and left the house in search of a flawless relationship. Then the supreme consciousness helped me abandon the material wealth. Whether earned or received, material wealth merely transfers hands. I realized this truth and so I am here to transfer it further."

"Papa," Avantika said, "fair distribution of wealth will surely settle the dispute among us but how to get rid of hurt feelings?"

"Let it go. That is the only answer, dear. We are imperfect human beings. Try and understand the imperfections of the other person and give them a chance to explain their side of the story. We project our insecurities onto others and in pursuit of doing so, become defensive. We don't even realize that we are becoming offensive to others. All of us are mingled in the vicious circle of life and death. Don't just keep reprimanding others. Being aware of the hurt feelings and then letting them go is the only way to reconciliation. The way to live in this world is to accept the people around you and direct your mind to amuse you in any phase of life. Staying with hurt feelings can never help you to grow. But learning to let go will surely make your life simpler and pleasant."

"It is easier said than done, Mr Lal," the judge spoke.

"Nothing in this world is impossible, My Lord. Wait for the divine call. With a materialistic mindset, things around us seem illusionary. Surrender your mind and be like a raw slate. Let the divinity enter you, you'll easily laugh at situations and let them go. It is merely the recognition of your divine call."

"But how do we recognize our divine call?"

"Just always feel blessed. Accept each situation of life as a part of his wish. He keeps sending his calls. Sometimes even a stone can turn your heart. Tulsidas recognized his divine call through his wife. Dacoit Vishwamitra became a saint after recognizing his divine call. I am the true example in front of you. The most difficult decision of my life, how to abandon my material wealth was made easy due to my divine call. I am blessed and privileged. Let all of us be blessed to recognize his voice."

Mr. Lal got up to leave the courtroom. Everyone stood up in gratitude.

"Where are you going, Papa?" his children asked.

"To serve his wish."

"But you can stay with us enjoy the rest of your life with your grandchildren."

"I am enjoying my life as never before, son. I have learnt to convert my attachments into detachments. My multimillionaire father will leave no worry for me. Let me stay in his supreme love. Your attachments toward this body are natural. But my soul is going to leave this cage one day. Till then, I wish to stay in realms of my beloved."

"Dad, we still need you. Don't you wish to stay with us?"

"Son, this soul is immortal and eternal. This body will not stay forever. Death is the final call but the soul will continue its journey in form of another body. This placement and replacement of bodies will continue till the time we attain the ultimate unity. He keeps blessing us with life to help us achieve supreme consciousness and to relish his bliss. Without a body it is impossible. So, to treat this body as a medium to rejoice the ecstasy of my beloved. Any departure from this kind of love will be treacherous to him. Let me be a stalwart and let me go."

There was a mesmerizing silence in the courtroom.

Satya Bhagat lifted his hands and the words flowed out of his mouth "Oh! Dear Lord, it was a sumptuous journey."

He thanked for the final verdict and left the courtroom.

Part II

Spiritual Discourses By Satya Bhagat

MAHA MANTRA – GAYATRI MANTRA

Why should we pray GOD? What should we ask from him in our prayers? Does GOD require any prayers? GOD is a reality and talking about realities time and again makes no sense for e.g., "The sun rises in the east." Since this is a world known reality, to say this repeatedly is hardly going to affect rising of the sun. Similarly, GOD is doing his job without any disturbance. Praying to GOD or praising him makes no difference to him. He offers his creation to every creature without any bias. GOD is already filled with happiness and bliss. So, how can praying to him make him happy? GOD is constantly pouring his grace to all living beings without any expectation or demands. He is filled with perfection, purity, and bliss. Does he require your offerings? Does he require places of worship to stay? He is all-pervasive, omnipotent, powerful, THE creator, sustainer and destructor of universe and dispenser of justice in relation to deeds attached to your soul. Why would he require any praises or prayers? Yet, we pray. WHY?

We pray because we, as humans, wish to share happiness and bliss with GOD. So, our prayers and praises to GOD do not necessarily affect him but it makes us feel blissful. We can sense our inner beauty only when we go near GOD. We pray to share the happiness which is obtained by connecting with GOD, to sense our inner beauty, and to realize the exceptional beauty of GOD.

There are billions of hymns in our scriptures that explain the concept of GOD and what should be asked from him while offering our prayers. One of such hymns is "Maha Mantra".

The mantra seems small but it has a deep meaning. Each word of the mantra can take years to be explained and understood.

A little explanation is given below:-

OM is the foremost word with which almost every hymn starts contains three letters. The first letter, denotes GOD. denotes soul. denotes PRAKRITI or nature. The three ever-present entities i.e. GOD, soul, and prakriti (nature) in this exact sequence are described in a single word.

It is the basic sound which is present in the universe. Even silence sounds like "OM." As God is ever present in every place, so he is called "OM." Vedic philosophers have different philosophies on the word "OM." There are endless names of GOD but "OM" is one name which contains all the meanings. When a child enters the world, it cries & makes sounds of "OM." Since it is the basic sound, it is used as the first word in all hymns.

"Bhur" literally means "Life of Lives." We are blessed with life and every part of our body is living. Your eyes can see because they have a life. Your tongue can taste because there is life in it. Your brains can think because it has got life in it. Your hands are functional because they are blessed with life. Your legs can walk because of their life. Each body part is working because of life. Blind people are not able to see because their eyes are lifeless. Deaf people cannot hear because their sense of hearing is lifeless. Any body part or any sense cannot work without life in that particular part. Therefore, this word "Bhur" in Gayatri Mantra has been described as the life of lives. This means we should be thankful to GOD that he has blessed us with life in all parts of our body. Had he made any one of these lifeless, life would have been hell. For a blind person, eyes are the most valuable thing in the world. But for a person who has got life in their eyes has no value for it. We must be grateful to GOD for blessing us with life and so he is called "life of lives."

"Bhuvah" means GOD is the one who removes our sufferings. GOD has given us the freedom to act and in that sense, we are the only cause of our sufferings. Just as if a son ignores his mother's advise while crossing the road and meets an accident, the mother cares for him to heal faster. Similarly, GOD helps us overcome the obstacles of life and helps in removing of the sufferings sooner & faster. We are bound with our karmic wheel & so ought to get fruits of our evil deeds. But GOD, as the remover of sufferings, helps us to forget the mishaps and to move ahead. He gives us the strength to face our problems. Apart from giving emotional & physical strength, GOD offers air, water, & plants in abundance for our use. He made trees, herbs, and insects for our wellbeing. He made seas, mountains, stars, sun, & moon for human beings. Anything created by GOD is purposeful and removes our sufferings in one sense or the other. GOD has left no stone unturned to provide us with the best. Even our insights, creativity, and intellect are given by GOD. So, GOD is best described as the "Remover of Sufferings."

"Swah" means GOD is the "Giver of Happiness." GOD created the universe just to give us happiness. We keep wandering from one place to another in search of happiness. But if we analyze properly, we can feel that happiness lies in everything GOD has given us. GOD is all pervasive and blissful, so, if there is no place without him, it means the entire universe is filled with happiness. GOD gave us such a beautiful body. This is one reason to be happy. He made such a wonderful world. This can be another reason to be happy. GOD has selflessly given everything to us. He made grass, plants, herbs, animals, trees, and insects to make us happy. He gave us a mind to materialize things for our happiness. He provided the raw materials to make us feel comfortable. He constantly pours his grace on us without any kind of expectation. If we are not able to understand his grace, it is our fault. GOD keeps showering his blessings on us. Whenever we feel depressed GOD comes to soothe us. In this sense, we look at GOD as the "Giver of Happiness."

"Tatta" is a Sanskrit word used in the auspicious hymn as a pronoun to describe GOD i.e. GOD who is the "Life of Lives," "Remover of Sufferings," and "Giver of Happiness"

"Savitah" is written in Gayatri Mantra as savitur, which means GOD is the creator and sustainer of the universe. GOD created this universe with the help of three ever-present constituents of (Prakriti) Nature which are Sattva, Rajas, and Tamas. He not only created the universe but he sustains it as well. Everything works in a perfect and disciplined manner. Days and nights come at their accurate times, the sun rises in the east and sets in the west, rivers flow at their pace, seasons change at their time, we grow older day by day and time runs ahead. The vicious circle of life and death keeps going on. GOD provides souls justice as per their deeds and sends them to their appropriate environment. All these jobs seem so difficult are as easy for GOD as the blinking of eyes. So, in this word I look at GOD as most powerful.

"Varenyam" means that such powerful GOD is the only one who should be followed with complete faith & devotion. Complete faith means dropping all ifs and buts, all doubts & worries, all fears & guilts, all the queries about things related to GOD. It means we should view such powerful lord with pure love. In this sense, the word denotes belongingness between GOD and soul. The soul should be surrounded by GOD in such a manner that there remains no difference between the both.

"Bhargah" means GOD is the biggest well-wisher of all the species. We have a small mind, narrow sight, and limited knowledge. We cannot judge if things that are happening are good or bad for us. GOD knows what is good or what is bad for us. Whenever we start doing something wrong, GOD fills our mind with fear & advises us to stop. Whenever we wish to do something good, he fills our heart with joy and enthusiasm. If we do something wrong by not listening to his advice, we feel grief and guilt. This guilty consciousness helps us repent & not repeat our mistakes. GOD helps us forget the past and to move further. The whole world may be against us, but he is always there to support, console and care for us. What we need is just to feel blessed always. What an amazing well-wisher he is! Just and merciful. He punishes us for our well being only. As soon as we finish with the punishment we are out of that mistake like a raw slate.

"Devasya" is segregated as Dev + sya. "Dev" denotes GOD and "Sya" is added to make the sentence grammatically correct. Literally, the word means "GOD" has all good features and wonderful qualities. He is the one who has created this universe, who always thinks for us, who is our biggest well-wisher, who is pure and perfect, who is exceptionally beautiful and wonderful, who is the single support of the universe, who is not bound by desires, who is merciful and blissful, who only gives and never demands, who is full of knowledge, who is extremely benevolent, who is generator, operator and destroyer, who is love himself. So this word denotes GOD possessing all wonderful qualities.

"Dhi Mahi" is segregated into two words. "Dhi" means "to owe" and "Mahi" means Me or I, so the word in total implies "I Owe." There is no other in the whole universe who is so beautiful and who always thinks for us. So I owe such beautiful GOD my heart, my mind, my senses, and my body. A sense of belongingness between soul and GOD is created. It explains the craving of the soul to meet GOD. When this kind of craving happens, the soul yearns to for a single glance of GOD. It explains the intensity of love when the soul wishes to owe Lord. The stronger the intensity, the sooner we attain communion with GOD. Owing Lord means there remains no difference between GOD and soul. When unconditional love is there, no doubts are there.

In continuation the whole phrase is like this:

"I owe the lord with all good features and wonderful qualities."

"Dhiyo Yo Nah":

This phrase of Gayatri Mantra is segregated into three sparate words. The first word (Dhiya) means intellect or intelligence. "Yo" denotes the pronoun used for GOD as you, and Nah means "Our." So, the literal meaning of the phrase is "You come in our intelligence." When the intensity of love, the craving to meet Lord reaches its peak and the soul actually contains LORD within itself, it prays, "Dear Lord, please come to my intelligence." Till the time we are working with our intelligence we tend to think we are always right. But when we call GOD to enter in our intelligence, it is complete surrender. In this stage of the mantra that self-realization takes place. With such unconditional love, surrender happens naturally and the soul wants GOD to work on its behalf.

"Pracho dayat," literally means, "You inspire me for good deeds." When the soul calls GOD in its intelligence and surrenders completely, it becomes pure. When GOD is working on our behalf, he inspires us to do good deeds only. When we surrender before GOD completely we reach the highest level of purity because now GOD is directing us.

Gayatri Mantra in its continuation is explained like this:

Dear LORD! Thou are "life of lives," "remover of sufferings," and "giver of happiness." Thou created the universe and sustain it with complete perfection. Thou only should be followed because thou are my biggest well-wisher endowed with all good features and wonderful qualities. I wish to owe thou in my mind, in my heart. I belong to you. Please enter in my mind to pure my intelligence and inspire me for good deeds. I completely surrender my intelligence to thou, so that I am saved from all evils.

Just reciting the mantra cannot help you achieve perfection, but analyzing and acting accordingly will take you near the Lord sooner. The auspicious hymn has the ability to purify you and so it is called MAHAMANTRA.

Learning starts as the life is conceived. The last breath is also the learning experience. Then why to stop learning in between?

Life in its true sense
Is not just to live
The way you want to live.
But it is a passage of transformation
From imperfection to completion
From the darkness to light
To choose what is wrong or right
Towards a ray of simple beauty
Towards the passion for thy duty
To thrive to be open to accept
To consider "giving up meekly" as a threat
To take challenges as opportunities
To transform the self and then the communities
To continue to work till hope is alive
With the dynamics of hope, life can strive
To reach the zenith of satisfaction
Come, Let's be responsible for our transformation.

- Peace is the freedom of mind where each living being is out of sufferings and is enjoying the state of highest dignity of existence.

It is being human and goes beyond humanity for any existing species on earth. It is the harmony of nature, the blend of colours, and a rainbow of joy where everything is balanced yet unique. It is the unconditional love that flows in the eternity; for everyone, for Peace is GOD himself.

- Discipline in life makes us more organized. Just as water within the boundaries of a river gives life, but the one with broken edges causes death..........Living in boundaries define our strength of character.

- Never tell your lord about the magnitude of your difficulties, rather tell the difficulties how magnificent your lord is!

- Love your SELF. That is the most neglected person in your life. Spend quality time with yourself. That's how depression cannot touch you. It's when you neglect your SELF, you feel depressed. So stay strong by loving it.....

- Why is it so easy to hold hurt feelings and so difficult to hold anger? It is because we are highly sensitive towards ourselves but not so sensitive to others. If we put ourselves in other's shoes we might realize their intentions. Every person has his\her side of the story. Behaviour can be defined........ Not judged or analysed.

- The beauty of life lies in sharing.
  Sharing joys with everyone.
  Sharing sorrows with your source.
  Sharing your skills with the needy.
  Sharing your knowledge with the world. With your limited sharing, you can reach the unlimited.............

- Connecting to your source is not that difficult. Just take two minutes after each hour and appreciate your lord. Practice this for a month and enjoy the transformation within yourself......... Stay connected.

- Anxiety is not bad till the time you're aware of it. So before your anxiety magnifies itself and turns into depression, recognize that you are big enough to handle it at a meagre stage. No problem is bigger than our SELF. It is due to the fact that the SELF exists, that the problem arises. Without SELF where is the problem? Strengthen yourself..............

- Prolonged anxiety can affect SELF learning process. Awareness can help in recognizing it.

- Forgiving is not easy. But it leads to inner freedom where the forbidden people haven't been given place to stay or are allowed to hurt you. Forgive others and free your SELF......

- Why do we crave for Gender equality? What do we wish to prove? Nature has separately defined all genders. It is about human equality. Each gender is human with undefined strengths. Rediscover your SELF in terms of humanity that is beyond gender. Gender belongs to the body. Your SELF is not affected by your gender unless you relate it..........by giving more importance to your gender.

- We authorize others to hurt us. But we choose to get hurt or to stay alert. People would surely talk with their own faculties. If your SELF is alert no one can make you feel hurt.

- Happiness is our nature. When we deviate from it, we crave for it. Then we search it by changing places, changing circumstances, etc. Just come back to your

SELF. Search for your source. Happiness lies there in form of bliss.....

- Immorality is irresistible. The faculties of mind push us towards negative things faster than positive things. Our SELF needs the training which can help us resist negativities. Just like the remote control of a T.V that is in our hand and we choose what channel we intend to see,
- the mind needs to be taken in SELF control.
- Silence and smile takes you inward. Expression takes you outward. The more you use your expression wisely and speak only when required, your SELF will gather strength. Your smile will become your nature.
- If you have done something wrong, admit it. But if you are right, and others think you are wrong - ignore it. They are free to think anything.
- One who trusts you will never demand an explanation. One who does not trust you will never trust your explanation. So why to explain unnecessarily?
- Living in harmony with your SELF leads to true happiness. It is impossible to make the world happy. When you're SELF content and not SELF contained you feel happy in any situation. Why depend on the world to be happy?
- Your SELF is your best friend. It is surrounded by your ego. Channelize your mind to confront your ego. Your will to accept your faults will naturally defeat your ego. Enjoy being your SELF.........free from ego.
- Ego is like a stubborn kid. The more you fulfil its demands, the more demanding it becomes. Ignore it and it will run after you. Your SELF should drive it, it should not drive your SELF. Feel the freedom by introspection. It is very easy to blame others and very difficult to realize

own mistakes. Just give 5 minutes to recall your daily routine before sleeping. Your awareness about your routine will indicate your mistakes. Admit your mistakes and learn not to repeat them. This will make your SELF feel the inner freedom...

- Your SELF is the reservoir of calmness. As your temptation towards the outside world diminishes, you feel calm and peace.

- When we are stressed, we feel suffocated. As the situation changes, we feel out of stress. That means we are affected by the situations. If we accept any situation with the mindset that all situations are variable and only my SELF is static with a dynamic mind. Then there will be less stress. A little stress, however, is not bad.

- It is easy to get carried away by the outer influences. With practice, your SELF can attain strength to not to be swayed by anything. Choose whether to let go or to hold a situation at will, because situations will change. Administer your SELF to float over the situations.

- Why do we worry so much about losing our identity? In that sense when we lose 'I', we gain our sense of SELF. People give us opportunities to see inward and gain the SELF. Gaining your SELF by losing your identity is worth it. Isn't it?

- Why is it difficult to accept your faults and apologize? To err is human and to apologize is humane. Accepting your faults give your SELF a wonderful opportunity to mortify your ego and release your heaviness. Free your SELF by accepting your faults.

- Life is not about collecting things. How much can we collect? Living life completely means fewer collections and so lesser problems. What we need is happiness.

Lesser your needs more will be your happiness. Let's be happy......

- The biggest challenge of life is to accept people as they are and respond to situations. When we are unable to view the viewpoints of the people around us, we tend to pose threat to our SELF, which becomes diseased. When we accept others we remain at ease. So being at ease or not is a matter of our choice.

- Equalizing is tranquillizing. It is difficult to respond to all situations with the same attitude but when we practice more to see all varied situations alike, we learn to be "drishta", just an onlooker. When we look at everything happening around us as "just a situation" and choose not to react, then we learn to equalize. It is like treating respect and disrespect alike or watching happiness and sorrow without affecting your SELF, you learn tranquillity. So, let's equalize.

- Situations are our best lessons. They teach us how to respond. Whether good or bad, they improve the immunity of our SELF. Appreciating or criticizing, the choice is ours. Let them teach and let's learn. Be calm and love whatever comes your way.

- Controlling emotions may lead to suffocation. Let the emotion work its way. Just be aware of its working. Watching your emotions will not suppress it but it will help you to understand it better. Enjoy your emotions. Just learn not to react to emotions. Emotions demand understanding, not the REACTION.

- What can be the best reaction to weird situations? Usually, we tend to lose our control. If we look at the situation as a passing affair, we can smile it off. SELF is static whereas situations are variable. Why let SELF be affected by altering variables. Let's learn to be static.

- Creativity is God's grace bestowed on you. Destruction is the ego's self-inflicted injury. A new creation fills everyone with gratitude. Destruction fills everyone with remorse. Due to some persons' ego, the society suffers a lot. Let us shed away this little demon, "ego", and live in grace.

- Complain less, compliment more.
  Tolerate less, accept more.
  Collect less, content more.
  Be SELF less, Enjoy the SELF more.

- Depression is the sign of losing your inner battle. If you want to win, strengthen your SELF by practising divinity. Divine strength would not let you lose.

- Depression can be treated by altering your situation. A change in situation leads to change in our minds. That means depression is a state of mind. If you are aware of your state of mind then why wait for situations to change? Treat it by affirmation, by telling your mind the strength of your SELF.

- Self-determination makes you really strong. "Arjun bhav." Just like Arjuna surrendered his chariot to Lord Krishna but was self-determined, surrender the intellect to the lord and be self-determined.

- Mythology depicts SELF as Arjuna, the warrior. Arjuna is strong yet emotional. He works with conviction and grace. He is also unwilling to accept circumstances as they are. He doubts himself while performing his duties. When things spiral out of his control, he surrenders. But he questions his Lord, by saying, "Dear Lord, It is really difficult to kill my own people. Why should I do such a heinous thing?"

- The Lord smiled and takes the chariot in the middle of the Warfield. The Lord wanted to show him the battle of contrasts, the world of opposites, the life with choices. He had only two options - either do it or leave it. One who enters to live exits to die. Matter leaves the body and assimilates with the matter. Lives go by till the time we don't realize the real purpose of the lives. We never cease to exist. Arjuna then asked, "if we never cease to exist, then why do we change forms?"

- The Lord smiled and replied, "The soul is unaffected by forms. Forms are illusions created by the ingredients (fire, water, air, space and earth) taken from nature. Your intellect can help you to differentiate between the real and the illusion, the form is an illusion and the soul is real. This form is given to the soul to realize it's the only purpose, that is the Communion between me and you. Without a form, you are in a dormant state. To get you into an active state, it was imperative to give you a form. Analyse your SELF as reality, away from any illusion. Come to me, I am life. Rest is death. Inactivity is escapism. To work is your duty. The work you decide for yourself is your battle. Each day you need to work to sustain in your war. Prayers without action are futile. Action with surrender is life… rest is death.

- What is God?

God is a concept. If a pot is there, a potter must have made it. Similarly, if the world exists, it's creator must be there. On the world map, we see many countries, we may not have seen them all. Yet they exist. Similarly, the concept of God can be accepted. Initial stages of understanding God as a concept is like telling a small kid about an object. For eg., an apple. How do you explain the concept of apple to the kid? By telling its features. It is a fruit, red in colour, and round. Similarly, we need to understand the features of God as a concept.

- What are the features of GOD?

God is real, eternal, blissful, omnipresent, omniscient, immortal, pure, compassionate, just, omnipotent, creator, operator, and destroyer of the universe. He is our biggest well-wisher, advisor and is all pervasive. No place is empty of him. He is static, yet dynamic.

- How can we realize GOD?

  Just as air is believed, God is to be believed. Our ancestors made some rituals, rules, and procedures to make us believe in God. They gave him a form. They wrote books which are to be read every day. They made routines that should be followed. Basically, they wanted us to understand and learn the concept of God. Just as children are taught a set pattern at school, we follow the rules and procedures to understand the concepts. So, Stage 1 to realize God is to follow a certain pattern to understand the concept.

- Once the pattern of understanding God as a concept is established and the concept turns into belief, ask yourself "Do I really know him?" Repeatedly ask this till the time your consciousness replies. As you get your answer, your belief turns into FAITH. This transition is the onset of Stage 2. Establish a relationship with God. Be it mother, father, sibling, friend, enemy, or beloved. No relationship needs rules or patterns. Similarly, the relationship between you and God is beyond rules and rituals.

- Stage 2 depicts God as formless, omnipotent, and omnipresent. It is a well-known fact that we generally connect with like-minded people. God being static, unable to change places as he is everywhere, connects to our SELF only when we become static. There static means to establish peace within our senses and mind. A peaceful mind can be obtained with practice. To let go of the hard feelings and smile over the situations. To mortify your ego and accept everything. To love whatever comes your way. All this is possible only when your heart is truly filled with love and surrender. So during this stage, each time is time for praying.

- Let's try to form a relationship with God. God as a mother:

Being the creator, God becomes our mother. The biggest womb in which the whole universe stays. GOD is always there to support, listen, help, and warn. He loves but not to spoil us. He soothes us in pain. He is a perfect blend of strength, strictness, calmness, and softness. When we form a relationship with him, we need to be like a child. A child holds his mother's finger while crossing the road. He is not bothered by the traffic on the road. Similarly, don't worry about the traffic during the journey of your life, just enjoy your walk. He can take care of us better than ourselves.

- We can form another relationship with God. As father: A father is someone who wishes you to grow until you reach the sky. He would listen to your problems without being judgemental. He is strict, yet soft. He is hard, yet simple. The well-wisher who expects nothing but the best for us. He punishes us for all wrongdoings. His strong hands surround us when we are scared. God, as father, surround us with his strength. Just feel blessed.

- Similarly, other relationships can be formed easily. The way you treat your brother, friend, beloved, or mentor, think of him the same way. Once this is achieved, you can reach Stage 3, where there is no difference between you and him. The realization that "All that was to be known, is known now," happens in this Stage.

- Letting go is not easy. We carry a burden of hurt feelings, grudges, regrets of past, and worries of the future with us. This is a wonderful life and we all are blessed with minds. Just convert this mind into intellect and observe the dynamic nature of SELF. Connect with your SELF by letting go of everything. It's truly amazing being burden free.

- We are static but the situations are dynamic. Time and situations are interrelated. Stop working on situations. Start working on your SELF. Understand the nature of situations and know your worth. SELF is beyond barriers, you can reach it with great ease. It's the only journey that's needed. Rest can be taken care of.

- The mind wanders till the time it feels blessed. Thoughts swirl in the mind and make us restless. This restlessness leads to tiredness. When we feel tired it becomes difficult to respond. So what's the solution? Empty your mind by just feeling blessed. As it happens, the thoughts will come to rest. An emptied mind is filled with gratitude. The smile naturally dances on the face.

- Life is full of suffering. Gratitude gives strength to live and bear these suffering. Material loss or emotional turmoil, gratitude helps us fight them all. Nothing can be bigger than SELF. Leave aside all fears and fill your SELF with gratitude. Your sufferings will come to an end.

- Sometimes nature offers such things which become difficult to accept. It is a human tendency that when you don't get what you want, you feel doubt. Simply be a spectator for some time. With time SELF would become mature in terms of accepting the happenings.

- Attachment is a state of mind. Detachment is the way to experience this life like a character being played. Had it been another body we would feel attached to relations related to that body. We feel attached to the time we don't surrender our attachments. Being aware of your attachments and their changing nature can take you back to your source.

- Anger is the sign of our inner weakness. When we expect things to happen our way and people to behave in a certain manner and it happens otherwise, we feel offended and thus feel angry. Anger is our manifestation of unfulfilled expectations. Let's give chance to people to work their way, leaving away the expectations.

- Jealousy is another weakness of our SELF. It is the result of comparisons. Everyone in this world has their share of plus and minus. We compare with the plus part and feel jealous. If we start comparing the minus part, we will be filled with gratitude. Gratitude strengthens the SELF. Don't be jealous. Live in gratitude. Love.......

- Over possessiveness is another sign of weakness and is caused due to insecurity. We don't realise that is actually putting the other person in the burden of our expectations. Giving space to our loved ones can create better relationships. Love means giving not demanding.

- When we look at the situations as an onlooker and witness the happenings, it becomes easy to practice detachment.

- Life is a beautiful gift. Each breath is important. Be wise in using the breaths. Lead a less stressful life. Strengthen your SELF to deal with your emotions.

- True happiness lies in being satisfied with what you have. This does not mean eschew working hard. Give your 100%, only then you will be able to feel free from the burden of inactivity. After that, contentment in what you have will give your SELF the inner freedom which leads to true happiness.

- Even when divine pleasure is so pure and untouched by any sorrow, we tend to run towards the worldly pleasures which are mixed with sorrows. After effect sorrow, the sorrow of expectations, and illusionary sorrows are attached to worldly pleasures but divine pleasure is limitless, unbounded, and pure. Then why do we run towards the worldly pleasures?

Our body is made of the ingredients taken from mother nature - earth, air, water, fire, and space. Our mind is proportionate to Sattva, Rajas, and Tamas. When our body and mind are made from mother nature, it is our natural tendency to run towards worldly pleasure. After all, a child clings to its mother.

- Our mind constitutes of Sattava, Rajas, and Tamas. The proportion is defined as per our karmas. However, we can alter the proportion through SELF analysis. Let's say a person' s mind is made up of 60% sattava, 30% rajas, and 10% Tamas. So, most of the times he will have a helpful nature: Satva guna. Even the food we eat affects our state of our mind. It is a scientific method to read minds. Once we are aware of our proportionate balance, we can control our emotions and strengthen our SELF.

- All worldly pleasures are mixed with sorrows. After-effect Sorrow: Eating in right quantity gives pleasure. Overeating leads to after effect sorrow. All sensory pleasures can be easily understood by this. One needs to learn SELF control to enjoy sensory pleasures.

- The next sorrow is mixed with the pleasure of attachment. Being attached to money, status, things, or people naturally calls for sorrow of expectations. Let go of the contrasting effects of attachment. Equate the contrasts and there will be no expectations. Be SELF content.

- The third type of sorrow attached to the worldly pleasure is the sorrow of illusion. We connect ourselves with this unreal world and keep ourselves in an illusion. If I drive, I will meet with an accident. If this happens then... If my loved ones die, then what... This sorrow of illusion is created by nature. Disillusion your SELF and enjoy the happenings. Leave the unreal and live with the real.....

- Economics of pleasure work upon the law of diminishing returns i.e with each increasing unit of pleasure, the satisfaction decreases, then comes to an end, and then further becomes negative. All the sorrows attached with worldly pleasure are the result of this law. So which is the pleasure that is an exception to this law?

- The divine pleasure - bliss is pure, unaffected by sorrow. Law of increasing returns is the economics of divine pleasure. Once the SELF tastes it, it can never forget it. The more you get into it the more you will relish it.

Happy Motherhood

- HOSTING A NEW LIFE

- Life is the most wonderful gift with which our planet is blessed. Most fortunate of all is to get life in a human body. In that, we are blessed more than any other creature on earth. No other creature can establish communion with GOD. Only human life uncovers the mysteries of GOD and the things made by him. GOD has given freedom and opportunity to the human life to reach happiness and bliss. In that sense, we are the most privileged souls on the planet earth. GOD is so perfect in the dispensation of justice that he gives life to souls according to their karmic orders. Each soul is born with the deeds which are the scriptwriters of its destiny.

- When the creator, God transferred his duties and responsibilities of creating to a woman, he arranged for the unborn life to get settled and to sustain itself in a small compartment. He arranged for proper nourishment of the baby in the mother's womb before it actually enters the world. So it is one of the major responsibilities of the expecting mother to host a new life in such a manner that the new life must feel privileged and special. But how should we host a new life?

- First of all, the biological parents of the child must plan to host a new life. When we go for an interview or to meet someone or in a formal/informal party, we plan our dress, our hairstyle, and our schedule accordingly. Then why the biggest responsibility of hosting a new life is not planned? Planning doesn't mean to plan the family according to your needs and requirements, it means to invite a new soul into the body. Should we let the new soul enter without preparing for it? When for a small interview we plan our entry and prepare for the expected questions then why don't we plan to host a new life?

- The body formation is based upon the reproduction system which on one hand gives sexual pleasure and on the other, gives entry to a new life. Mere sexual gratification and the act done without thinking nullifies the very purpose of hosting the new life. The physical, mental, and spiritual growth of the unborn depends upon the expecting mother's psychology. In order to make a complete and balanced human being a new life must be hosted with piousness. Each soul is bound by his/her Karmic wheel. When a soul is invited by parents, God sends the soul in accordance with the capabilities of the parents. So, before inviting a new soul the parents must prepare themselves. Keep a check on your daily routine, on your diet, and on your lifestyle. Prepare yourself for inviting a pious soul in your body. Keep your thoughts clear and call the soul, while engaged in the sexual act. The purpose of the act is to host a new life, to welcome a pure soul in the body. Make it auspicious because its purpose is pure.

- After welcoming a new soul into the body, bid thanks to the creator for choosing you as a transmission channel for the new soul. He has given you the most wonderful job -

creation. Expecting parents are the most blessed people because they are helping God by creating a new life. What an exceptionally beautiful feeling! So, now that a new life has entered the body, the mother becomes responsible for its physical, emotional, mental, and spiritual growth and development. When you take responsibility of hosting a new life you may feel biological and emotional changes in your body. The reason is simple and clear. You are nurturing a soul bound by its Karmic wheels and the unborn mindset of past incarnations can affect your system. This is the reason for the mood swings you feel when you are expecting. So host a new life with clear thoughts, purity, and devotion to God.

द्वन्द (मन व आत्मा)

मनोवाच :
मैं चंचल मैं विचलित
मैं अस्थिर मैं द्रवित
मैं भवविभोर मैं मलिन
मैं अठखेलियों भरा
मैं अल्हड निरा
मैं अति विशाल
मैं अपनी ही ढाल

कैसे मुझ में कोई रंग ढले
कैसे मुझ में विश्वास पले
कोई मुझसे ना जीत सके
जब चल जाऊ अपनी मैं चाल

मैं उड़त फिरत
यूँ ही भटकत
अपने ही गगन में रहूँ विचरत
कोई कैसे मेरी और बडे
कोई कैसे मुझसे आगे चले
मुझ से बडा ना कोई है ठग
मैं हूँ विपरीत तो डरे है काल

मैं ज्वलंत रहूँ मैं सजग दिखत
मैं चारों दिशा की सैर करत
मेरा ना कोई माप धरे
मुझसे सम्पूर्ण विश्व डरे
जब फैलाऊँ अपना मैं मायाजाल

तू निकल सके तो रहा निकल
तू फसत जात मैं हसत जात
मैं फिर जीता तू फिर हारा
अब हार तू स्वीकार कर

है हिम्मत तो फिर से लड़
आ देख करूँ क्या मैं तेरा हाल

आत्मा ऊवाच :
ओ बांवरे मन , यूँ ना दे मिसाल
तू है अशव, मैं तेरा घुड्साल
तू दिशा हीन मैं तेरी मशाल
तू मेरे हाथों की कठपुतली
जब मैं चाहूँ तब रखे तू ताल

हाँ ! मेरा अहम निकम्मा है
तेरी भाषा में बोले बोल
पर आ खोलूँ मैं तेरी पोल
जब अहम बुद्धि के पास चला
तब तेरा क्या रह गया भला

तुझमे मुझमे ना कोई अंतर
यदि मैं नहीं तो नहीं तेरा कोई घर
इस घर में अगर तू रहना चाहे
तो जो मैं चाहूँ वो तू कर
तू सजग रह और अडिग रह
मत अहम को आने दे भीतर
फिर तू और मैं मिल ज़ायेंगे
तब बन जाना तू मेरी ढाल
मैं अति सूक्षम तू अति विशाल
मैं अति सूक्षम तू अति विशाल

Feel connected always. You are never alone. Relish what comes your way with love, acceptance, conviction, and grit. Have faith and courage to convert your challenges into opportunities. Live fully and transcend into the serenity of SELF.